Nice words about a nice
person, Harriet Welling

Paul M. Angle

A Portrait of Abraham Lincoln

Isaac Markens

Robert Todd Lincoln

A PORTRAIT OF

Abraham Lincoln

IN LETTERS

BY HIS OLDEST SON

Edited by PAUL M. ANGLE

with the assistance of Richard G. Case

THE CHICAGO HISTORICAL SOCIETY

CHICAGO, ILLINOIS

Publication of this book was made possible by the
PHILIP K. WRIGLEY FUND

INTRODUCTION

Two YEARS AGO the Chicago Historical Society acquired a series of eighty-two letters written by Robert Todd Lincoln, and in a few instances, his secretaries, to a retired journalist, Isaac Markens, between 1903 and 1926. The letters make no startling revelations, yet they throw enough light on aspects of the life of Abraham Lincoln and on the character and personality of his son to justify their publication. (A few purely perfunctory letters have been omitted.)

In 1905 Isaac Markens, then in his fifty-seventh year, was a broker on the New York Cotton Exchange. His early career had been varied. Having only a public school education, he had started to work, in the shipping and commission business, at the age of sixteen. After several years he became a traveling salesman. He then learned stenography and worked for four years for the Pennsylvania Railroad. In 1881 he was appointed assistant manager of the United Press Association. Thirteen years of newspaper work followed—on the staffs of the *New York Commercial Advertiser*, the *New York Mail and Express*, and the *New York Star*.

In 1887, while working for the *Mail and Express*, Markens wrote a series of articles on the Jews in America. The response of readers led him to expand the articles into a 352 page book which he published himself in 1888: *The Hebrews in America; A Series of Historical and Biographical Sketches*. The opening sentences set the tone of the work: "With a population of only 400,000 in the entire country, of which number 125,000 are credited to New York, the Hebrews have made themselves felt throughout the land to an extent far greater than any other like number of people. . . . Enterprising and foremost in all public movements looking to the welfare of the entire community, patriotic and law-abiding, cosmopolitan in their charities, and permitting none of their people to become a burden on the state or city, their presence is welcomed and their power is extending year after year." The book is replete with detail but it lacks documentation and is poorly organized. Nevertheless, it was a pioneer effort and continues to be of some value.

In 1894 Markens retired from newspaper work and for the rest of his life made a living, probably not a very lucrative one, on the Cotton Exchange. However, it is evident, from his letters and from the statements of those who knew him, that historical scholarship was his primary interest.

What led Markens to initiate a correspondence with Robert Lincoln can only be conjectured. Perhaps, in 1903, the New Yorker was already contemplating the series of Lincoln studies he would begin to publish six years later. At any rate, he asked Robert Lincoln for his own photograph, and received a perfunctory reply dated February 9, 1903: "In reply to your letter of January 13th, I regret that I have not a satisfactory photograph of myself to use in complying with your request." If Markens appealed to Lincoln again during the next five years the latter's replies have not survived, which seems unlikely. With the resumption of correspondence in 1908 Robert Lincoln's first letters, though polite, were not encouraging, but Markens persisted. After a few years Lincoln let down his reserve and revealed his true self.

By 1903 Robert Todd Lincoln, then in his sixtieth year, had reached the peak of his career. He had a lucrative law practice in Chicago and counted many large corporations among his clients. In 1881 Garfield appointed him Secretary of War, and Arthur kept him in office after Garfield's death. The country was at peace and the military establishment small, so the Secretary of War had little opportunity to distinguish himself. Lincoln seems to have had little enthusiasm for public office, but in 1889, when President Harrison appointed him Minister to England, he dutifully accepted. He filled the post competently, but with his usual reticence made few public appearances and kept out of the newspapers. The London years brought sorrow to him and Mrs. Lincoln with the death of their only son, Abraham Lincoln, in 1890.

One of Robert Lincoln's principal clients was the Pullman Company. When George M. Pullman died in 1897 Robert Lincoln became the company's chief executive, and soon afterward, its president. In 1911 failing health led him to resign. The following year he moved to Washington. For the remainder of his life he divided his time between that city and his summer home, "Hildene," at Manchester, Vermont.

Between 1909 and 1913 Isaac Markens published four studies of aspects of the life of Abraham Lincoln, all printed for the author in small editions. The first, occasioned by the Lincoln Centenary in 1909, was *Abraham Lincoln and the Jews*, a sixty-page booklet. The author had scanty materials to work with, but did a creditable job with what he had. In 1911 Markens published two slight pamphlets: *Why Lincoln Spared Three Lives*, and *President Lincoln and the Case of John Y. Beall*. The first related three instances of Lincoln's clemency toward Confederates; the second dealt with a sensational case in which the President refused to commute the death sentence of a prominent Confederate officer convicted as a spy.[1] Markens had witnessed the execution of Beall, which may account for his interest in the subject. Neither pamphlet can be called a contribution. Markens' last published writing,[2] a twenty-six page pamphlet entitled *Lincoln's Masterpiece: A Review of the Gettysburg Address New in Treatment and Matter*, 1913, was inspired by the fiftieth anniversary of the address. Although Robert Lincoln praised it, the pamphlet is superficial and falls short of the claim made in its subtitle.

Between 1908 and 1913, when Markens was concerned with these writings, he received only five letters from Robert Lincoln, so it is not strange that there are only two published references to the correspondence. The first occurs in *Abraham Lincoln and the Jews*, where Markens wrote: "Hon. Robert T. Lincoln states in reply to an inquiry of the writer, that he had 'never before heard that his father supposed he had any Jewish ancestry.'" The second reference comes in *Lincoln's Masterpiece*, in which Robert Lincoln's assertion, "I know of no opinion of my father himself on the Gettysburg Address," is quoted.

1. See beyond, p. 4, n. 3.
2. An obituary article in the *Publications of the American Jewish Historical Society* for 1931 credits Markens with a work entitled *Origin of Famous Lincoln Sayings*, 1918. *Who Was Who in America, 1897-1942* also lists this title among Markens' publications. If it does exist, it has not found its way into the standard bibliographies and library catalogs.

Why, after 1913, did Markens continue to press Robert Lincoln for information? Two probable reasons can be advanced. By this time Markens had become so interested in the Lincoln story that his curiosity was insatiable. And in all likelihood, he was gathering material for another book. Memorial articles in the *Publications of the American Jewish Historical Society* for 1931 and in the *American Hebrew* for September 14, 1928 both state that at the time of his death he was preparing a detailed work on Lincoln which was practically ready for publication. In fact, Emanuel Hertz, author of the *American Hebrew* article, was explicit on this point. "Toward the end of his life," Hertz wrote, "he prepared from his endless investigations a formidable volume in some thirty chapters—new incidents and recollections, minor details and hitherto unrecorded events which the ordinary author never stumbled upon but which are indispensable in the collections of everything new about Lincoln. It was my good fortune to have read the manuscript but I fear that his death may interfere with its publication, for age had somewhat interfered with the diction and sequence of events in this, his last effort, and he had no opportunity to put it in final shape for publication." The book was never published, and a diligent search has not brought the manuscript to light.

Few men in American history have been more misunderstood than Robert Todd Lincoln. For this there are several reasons. Because of his mother's widely publicized aberrations after his father's death, he cringed at publicity.[3] The tragic role the law compelled him to play in the commitment of Mary Todd Lincoln in 1875 was widely misinterpreted, and he took the blame for an unfilial if not a cruel act. Because he was aloof and retiring, he was accused of being a snob. For years he seldom gave out information about his father, and incurred the charge of being in-

3. An interesting instance of his aversion to public notice is to be found in the following letter to James Keely, editor of the *Chicago Tribune*, Chicago, June 22, 1903: "My dear Sir: I have your request for a modern photograph of myself for occasional use in the *Tribune*. I read the *Tribune* daily and it is one of the minor pleasures of life left to me that I can open the paper feeling sure that I am not to be confronted by a portrait of myself. I am so loath to lose this that I beg you will excuse my not complying with your request. Very truly yours, Robert T. Lincoln." Original letter in the library of the Chicago Historical Society.

different to Abraham Lincoln's life and reputation. The general public attributed his two appointments to public office as posthumous tributes to his father rather than to his own merits. As general counsel of the Pullman Company at the time of the strike of 1894 he found himself execrated by labor. In general, he has been considered a small man, mean, and cold.

Robert Lincoln's letters to Isaac Markens dispel many of these misconceptions. Aloof he was, but not a snob. If he had been, would he, an eminent public figure, have written dozens of letters to an obscure, retired newspaperman of Jewish ancestry? Unwilling to supply information about his father? The letters which follow show that he often took considerable trouble to answer Markens' inquiries. Indifferent to his father's reputation? Robert Lincoln battled fiercely to keep Abraham Lincoln's name unsullied, as many letters in this collection testify. And withal he was a kind man, patient, and generous.

PAUL M. ANGLE

Letters to Isaac Markens, Esq.
from
Robert Todd Lincoln

PULLMAN BUILDING, CHICAGO

May 19th, 1908

Isaac Markens, Esq.
    107 Pearl Street
    New York, N.Y.

Dear Sir:

Your letter of May fifteenth to Mr. Lincoln is received by him just as he is arranging to leave the office to take a train for the east, and in reply he directs me to say that while he has his own well-defined opinion of the motives which actuated both Herndon and Lamon in the extraordinary malice exhibited by them to the memory of their old friend,[1]* he does not care to write about it.

Yours very truly,
Chas S. Sweet
Secretary

1. The reference, of course, is to *Herndon's Lincoln, The True Story of a Great Life,* by William H. Herndon and Jesse William Weik (Chicago, 1889), and Ward Hill Lamon, *The Life of Abraham Lincoln, from His Birth to his Inauguration as President* (Boston, 1872). Herndon had been Lincoln's law partner from 1844 to 1861; Lamon was Lincoln's law partner in Danville, Illinois, after 1852, and was marshal of the District of Columbia, by Lincoln's appointment, from 1861 to 1865.

PULLMAN BUILDING, CHICAGO

December 21st, 1908

Dear Sir:

In reply to your inquiry of December 18th, I am sorry that I cannot give you any information. I have nothing but the general knowledge pos-

*Notes and references follow after each letter and are numbered consecutively.

sessed by all the public of the work of the Messrs. Seligman during the War, and never heard my father speak of the matter.[2]

Very truly yours,
Robert T. Lincoln

Isaac Markens, Esq.
New York Cotton Exchange
New York, N.Y.

2. Eight Seligman brothers, Bavarian-born Jews, founded the international banking house of J. & W. Seligman in New York City in 1862. The firm has been credited with selling United States bonds to the amount of $200,000,000 in Europe during the Civil War.

201 PULLMAN BUILDING, CHICAGO

March 23rd, 1910

My dear Sir:

In reply to the inquiry contained in your letter of March 16th, I can only say to you that I have never had any personal knowledge of the Beall case. As a youth I heard of it through the newspapers as other people did, and Messrs. Nicolay and Hay's work contains all that I know about it now.[3]

Very truly yours,
Robert T. Lincoln

Isaac Markens, Esq.
New York Cotton Exchange
New York, N.Y.

3. John Yates Beall, Confederate naval officer, was the leader in a scatter-brained plot to seize the Union warship *Michigan* on Lake Erie and with her liberate Confederate prisoners held on Johnson's Island at the entrance to Sandusky Bay. The plot, attempted in the fall of 1864, failed. A few weeks later Beall was arrested in up-state New York, and charged with being a spy and with violating the laws of war. He was tried and sentenced to death. Great pressure was brought on Lincoln to commute

4

Beall's sentence but the President would do no more than ask that Beall be given a few extra days to prepare for death. He was hanged on February 24, 1865. Markens wrote of the Beall case in his pamphlet, *President Lincoln and the Case of John Y. Beall*, privately printed in 1911.

HILDENE, MANCHESTER, VERMONT

Oct 8, 1913

Isaac Markens, Esq.

My dear Sir:

Herewith your letter for convenience of reply. My reply to your 1st question is negative. I do not think I ever knew anything about English opinion as to the Address.

Your 2d question refers I suppose to *"The Perfect Tribute,"* by Mrs. Andrews. It is of course a very charming fiction. Mrs. Andrews told me that she was inspired to write by the questions of her little son in consequence of an address of his school teacher. In her book, Mrs. Andrews erred in adopting the story that the Gettysburg address was hastily written on a scrap of paper on a train.

Very truly yours,

Robert T. Lincoln

HILDENE, MANCHESTER, VERMONT

Nov. 1st 1913

My dear Sir:

I thank you for your note. You have perhaps come across another proof of the wisdom of the advice, "Never burn a letter & never write one." I shall of course not use your name & would be glad to know more of the letter and its whereabouts. Can you not send me a copy of your copy? I should be much obliged.[4]

Very truly yours,

Robert T. Lincoln

4. This communication remains a mystery to the editor.

HILDENE, MANCHESTER, VERMONT

November 5th 1913

Isaac Markens, Esq.
My dear Sir:

In reply to your inquiry, I know of no expression of opinion by my father himself on the Gettysburg Address. I was in Washington shortly after its delivery, and he read to me the note from Mr. Everett which is at page 11 of a reprint of an article by Mr. Nicolay, a copy of which I am sending to you.[5] He indicated the pleasure given him by Mr. Everett's note,[6] but I do not think that he commented upon the speech. I am quite sure that I would remember anything of the kind. It is, I think, an indication that he was not greatly dissatisfied with it, that he wrote so many copies of it with his own hand.

I thank you for your other letter, as to which I will write you later, after a little research I am making. I shall not, be assured, use your name in any way.

Very truly yours,

Robert T. Lincoln

5. *Lincoln's Gettysburg Address*, reprinted from *The Century Magazine*, February, 1894.
6. On November 20, 1863, Edward Everett, the orator of the day, wrote to Lincoln: "I should be glad if I could flatter myself that I came as near to the central idea of the occasion in two hours as you did in two minutes." To which Lincoln replied on the same day: "In our respective parts yesterday you could not have been excused to

6

make a short address, nor I a long one. I am pleased to know that, in your judgment, the little I did say was not entirely a failure."

HILDENE, MANCHESTER, VERMONT

Nov. 6th, 1913

Isaac Markens, Esq.
My dear Sir:

There is no reason for my wishing to suppress my statement about Herndon, as I have no doubt of its truth. I ought perhaps to have qualified the word employment by adding the words "involving responsibility."

My father did offer him a membership on a temporary board of *three* persons—wage five dollars perday—to pass on war supply claims. I suppose the idea was that he could not do much harm, having two decent men to do the work. I think Herndon himself recorded the offer in one of his "works" but just now I cannot lay my hand on the place.[7]

With thanks for your interest I am,

Very truly yours,
Robert T. Lincoln

7. While Herndon did not seek an appointment early in Lincoln's administration, failing finances impelled him to appeal to his former partner in the winter of 1862–63. Lincoln offered him a position, at five dollars a day, on a commission to investigate cotton claims. Herndon declined. David Donald, *Lincoln's Herndon* (New York, 1948), pp. 153–56.

In a letter, dated July 26, 1918, to Emily Helm, half-sister of Mary Todd Lincoln, Robert Lincoln made this comment: "I was very glad to have your recent letter with its newspaper clipping in regard to my father's mother, Nancy Hanks. As you know, the blackguard Herndon after my father's death in revenging himself for being prevented by his drunken habits from receiving any Government patronage, conceived the idea of casting all sorts of aspersions upon Nancy Hanks. In his first book, he said that she was never married to her husband. This lie being quickly disposed of not only by the testimony of then living witnesses of her marriage, but by the discovery of a regular certificate thereof in the proper county clerk's office, Herndon then concluded to tell a lie which depended solely upon his personal statement. It was that while riding with my father one day, my father said to him that his mother was illegitimate. . . . Herndon's outrageous lie, for it was nothing else of course, has been perpetuated in a recent much noted Life of my father by Lord Charnwood in England." Original letter in the library of the Chicago Historical Society.

1775 N STREET, WASHINGTON, D.C.

February 1st, 1914

Isaac Markens, Esq.
My dear Sir:

I have at last received your "Lincoln's Masterpiece," and have read it with great pleasure.[8] I think it unlikely that the reports of the circumstances attending any public address,—its composition, its delivery, its reception by those who heard it and later by those who read it, —were ever before more carefully and thoroughly examined and placed on record together. The labor and zeal you have put into your work constitute in themselves a remarkable addition to the testimonials of admiration for the Gettysburg Address.

My attention had never before been called to your suggested possible influence of phrases in Mr. Everett's Oration; and your great enlargement of the list of prior users of the now familiar words at the close, is most interesting.

I am glad that you have made this important addition to the Gettysburg Address literature and thank you for your kindness in sending me a copy.

Believe me,
Very truly yours,
Robert T. Lincoln

8. See Introduction, p. xi

HILDENE, MANCHESTER, VERMONT

August 17, 1914

Isaac Markens, Esq.
My dear Sir:

I find to my regret that I have omitted to reply to your inquiry about a supposed dove of Peace having flown away from the beginning of the Gettysburg speech.[9]

Who in the world says he heard the sentence? With all the evidence as to the written sheets used at the time, the stenographic reports of all the news reporters & the careful accounts of trustworthy persons like Nicolay & Colonel Hay the story is ridiculous.

Omitting criticism of the style of the apochryphal phrases, it must have been absurd as material of the situation. In November 1863 the helmet of Mars was not open for war as a dove's nest. General Grant's Wilderness campaign & General Sherman's Georgia campaign were still in the future.

Sincerely yours,
Robert T. Lincoln

9. One of the many Lincoln myths has it that as the President rose to speak a dove, symbolic of peace, fluttered into the air.

.

1775 N STREET, WASHINGTON, D.C.

March 15, 1915

Isaac Markens, Esq.
My dear Sir:

I shall be glad to have a copy of your article on the Gettysburg speech.

I do not think that it is possible to give you any information about it which I do not know you to have already.

As to the various autograph copies made by my father, I can only add to the information contained in Mr. Nicolay's article (enclosed) by saying that there is a copy in John Hay's papers, which I fancy is a revision not adopted in the revision work spoken of by Nicolay. This paper is now no doubt in the Hay papers now in the hands of William Roscoe Thayer, who is preparing a life of Hay.

It is very odd that no trace can be found of the draft used at Gettysburg, so fully described by Nicolay.

Miss Nicolay knows nothing of it, & Mr. Richard Watson Gilder was unable to get anything from the archives of the Century Company, and it is not among my father's papers.

As to surviving persons, I can think only of Wayne MacVeagh who has been publicly quoted already & Col. Clark E. Carr, who long ago published a small book.[10]

Very truly yours,
Robert T. Lincoln

10. Wayne MacVeagh, district attorney for Chester County, Pennsylvania, in 1863, was one of those who accompanied Lincoln to Gettysburg. Later, he had a distinguished career in politics and public office. Clark E. Carr, of Galesburg, Illinois, represented his state on the Gettysburg Cemetery Commission. In 1906 he published a small pamphlet entitled *Lincoln at Gettysburg*.

HILDENE, MANCHESTER, VERMONT

June 21st, 1915

Isaac Markens, Esq.
Dear Sir:

In reply to your note, I never before heard of the alleged statement credited by you as being made by President Lincoln to some pastor.[11] Personally I give no credence whatever to what you describe as, "widely published" statements unless some trustworthy authority can be given. My old secretary, now deceased, used to amuse himself greatly in tracing the origin of such things and it was curious to see how many times he succeeded in locating the actual original faker.

Dr. Gurley was the pastor of the Presbyterian church which my father attended. He was not an "Illinois clergyman." If I was interested in tracing the authenticity of the quotation you give I should look up Dr. Gurley's writings and sayings, some of which I think could be found in Washington.

Very truly yours,
Robert T. Lincoln

11. The reference is to a statement attributed to the Rev. Dr. Phineas D. Gurley, pastor of the New York Avenue Presbyterian Church in Washington, where Lincoln attended services. In essence, Doctor Gurley was reported to have said that Lincoln intended to profess his faith in Christianity, but was killed before he could carry out his intention. See p. 12, n. 12.

HILDENE, MANCHESTER, VERMONT

June 28th, 1915

Isaac Markens, Esq.
My dear Sir:

An acknowledgement of your letter has been delayed by my absence from home. Using your references I find in the volume published at Springfield, Illinois, relating to the Lincoln Centennial Commemoration there, the report of the address of the Rev. Dr. Logan which I did not hear personally but read upon publication of the volume. I had forgotten his reference to Dr. Gurley; as to that, he does not specify when or where or how Dr. Gurley made the utterance cited by him.[12] I do not remember meeting Dr. Logan at Springfield but it occurs to me that he may possibly be still living and in charge of the congregation now occupying the old Presbyterian church in which was our family pew for many years.

From the way in which you speak of Dr. Logan's, "four column address," it occurs to me that perhaps you do not possess the volume in which it was published and I am therefore sending you one under a separate enclosure. If you have not seen the full address it will interest you, I am sure, to know what he says of Dr. James Smith, who is well known to me. Dr. Gurley was the distinguished pastor of the Presbyterian church in Washington which my father attended and it would be quite impossible to doubt the sincerity of an utterance of his if its authenticity was established. I do not recall the fact but I would not be surprised to know that Dr. Gurley had in his lifetime published a volume of memoirs; if so it could be found in the Library of Congress.[13]

Very truly yours,

Robert T. Lincoln

12. The Rev. Dr. Thomas D. Logan, pastor of the First Presbyterian Church of Springfield, Illinois, spoke on the subject, "Lincoln the Worshiper," at the Lincoln centennial observances at Springfield on February 12, 1909. There he made this statement: "His [Lincoln's] pastor, Dr. Gurley, said that the reports as to the infidelity of Mr. Lincoln could not have been true of him while at Washington, because he had frequent conversations with the President on these subjects, and knew him to be in accord with the fundamental principles of the Christian religion. He further declared that, in the latter days of his chastened life, after the death of his son Willie, and his visit to the battlefield of Gettysburg, he said, with tears in his eyes, that he had lost confidence in everything but God, that he believed his heart was changed, that he loved the saviour, and that if he was not deceived in himself, it was his intention soon to make a profession of religion." William J. Wolf, in *The Religion of Abraham Lincoln* (New York, 1963) called this asseveration "a dramatic overstatement."

13. Doctor Gurley left no memoirs.

HILDENE, MANCHESTER, VERMONT

July 7th, 1915

My dear Sir:

I return to you the letter of the grandson of Dr. Gurley which I have read with interest. It would seem that so far as Dr. Gurley is concerned the matter rests upon hearsay and I am old enough to give little confidence to hearsay stories, especially as to any exactness of circumstances or language. The letter of Mr. Gurley which I return indicates that his grandfather left no Memoirs or publications known to his grandson which would be useful in this connection.

I thank you very much for your articles relating to the Confederate Spies cases and the Beall Case which I have read with interest; your researches add, of course, greatly to my general remembrance of these matters. I shall have great pleasure in keeping the papers.

Very truly yours,
Robert T. Lincoln

Isaac Markens, Esq.

THE PULLMAN COMPANY, CHICAGO, ILLINOIS
OFFICE OF THE CHAIRMAN

November 8th, 1915

Isaac Markens, Esq.
    1061 St. Nicholas Avenue
    New York City
My dear Sir:

Your letter of November 2nd reaches me here, via Washington and Manchester, Vermont, hence my delay in acknowledging it.

I think that in consequence of correspondence you have become possessed of all my knowledge and ideas in regard to the Gettysburg speech, but if it does not delay your printing, and you care to have me do so, I will be very glad to look over the manuscript, if you will kindly send it to me to Manchester, Vermont. I shall not, however, arrive there before the end of this week. It is my expectation to remain there another month before going to Washington.

I did see in the papers some account of the sale of the Burton collection, but have no special knowledge regarding its items and did not know that one of my old letters was one of them. I do not remember at all what I wrote to Mr. Brooks,[14] but I have no idea that I said anything which I would wish to recall.

I am very much interested in what you say about the new publication, I do not think that I had before heard of it and I shall naturally be very much interested in it, for I am sure that I should be gratified by the feelings of its author.[15]

Very truly yours,
Robert T. Lincoln

14. Noah Brooks, Washington correspondent of the *Sacramento Union* during the Civil War, whom Lincoln intended to appoint as his private secretary in place of John G. Nicolay, who had submitted his resignation just before the President's death. In his later life Brooks wrote several books about Lincoln.

15. A reference to one of Markens's projected writings?

HILDENE, MANCHESTER, VERMONT

November 20th, 1915

Isaac Markens, Esq.
My dear Sir:

Referring to my letter of November 8th, I was detained in Chicago several days longer than I expected by a slight illness, the effect of which has not yet entirely passed off. I have not, therefore, been able to give as close attention to your manuscript as I would like; I have, however, read it with some care and return it herewith.

You have certainly made a most exhaustive research into all matters of interest concerning the Gettysburg Address and I am very glad to learn from your work, many things that I never heard of before.

I have ventured to attach, at page 27, the omitted paragraph of my letter to President Taft which I think important to be in if any extract from my letter is desirable.

I am much struck by the large addition of precedents for the expression of the thought in the last line of the Address.

I am also impressed by the new development of stories concerning the writing of the Address on the car and at Gettysburg, having in mind

14

Mr. Nicolay's clear statements confirmed by the lithograph of the Address.

One is struck with amusement at the stories you record; what, for instance, became of the Curtin copy of the envelope notes? Retirement to work in a room of the railway car is interesting when I, for one, know that no railway passenger car had a room at that date. Mr. Will's story of lending ink is also interesting; if anything is clear it is that the ink part of the manuscript was written in the White House and the second page in pencil at Mr. Will's house; the collection of anecdotes of this detail illustrates the value of the details of history.

I trust you will excuse me for calling your attention to the manuscript; it seems to have had some proof-reading, but it needs a very great deal more. I have called attention in pencil to only a few of the things that require typographical correction.

I would express myself more at length as to the pleasure I have had in the manuscript if I were quite well enough to do so.

Very truly yours,
Robert T. Lincoln

HILDENE, MANCHESTER, VERMONT

November 26th, 1915

Isaac Markens, Esq.
My dear Sir:

I have your letter of the 22nd inst. in regard to your Gettysburg article.

It does not seem to me that there is as much discrepancy in the matter of the copies of the Address as you suggest; I, myself, think the story is a very simple one; omitting all preliminary notes of which there is no record, I think my Father took with him to Gettysburg, the Address written in ink, probably upon two sheets of letter-paper, and having arrived at Gettysburg he concluded to change the last three words of the first page and all that followed them, and that this change was physically made in pencil on what became the second page of the Address as he had it in hand for delivery. Upon returning from Gettysburg, in order to reply to Mr. Everett's request, he made his revision which Nicolay says has become the standard. Probably during this process, he made a tentative revision which may be the one he gave to Colonel Hay; I have never seen it and do not know how exactly it agrees with the Baltimore version. You speak of this Hay copy as being made before my Father went to, "Washington;" I fancy this is a slip of your pen for "Gettysburg." I cannot think on what basis you suggest that the Hay copy was made before going to Gettysburg.

Your statement that my Father gave to Colonel Hay the two-sheet version, partly in pen and partly in pencil, and that it is now in the possession of Mrs. Wadsworth, startles me very much; I have for years been trying to trace that manuscript. I did not communicate with Mrs. Hay personally, but Miss Nicolay did and Miss Nicolay wrote me that Mrs. Hay had a complete ink version of the Address, but that she did not have the ink-pencil version. If you are correct this clears up what has long been a mystery to me; Mr. Gilder of the Century hunted high and low for it for me, it having been considered possible that it had not been returned to Mr. Nicolay after being lithographed. I shall be much interested in talking this over with Mrs. Wadsworth this winter.

Mr. Nicolay says in his article that my Father made probably half a dozen or more copies after the Everett copy; I am surprised that one of them was not owned by Mr. Nicolay and found in his papers, but Miss Nicolay says there is no trace of it.

It seems to me that the use of the word, "standard," by Mr. Nicolay explains itself; he says that my Father made a version for Mr. Everett which has become the standard and he then says that he made a copy of that for the Baltimore Fair and of this he says, that this by frequent publication has properly become the standard text. There is no indication that the Baltimore version is not exactly like the Everett version and, as to that, Mr. Nicolay says if in any respect the later copies differ, it was due to accident and against my Father's intention.[16]

Merely one word about the room in the car; I have always understood that the car to Gettysburg was an ordinary passenger car of the time, so I think it is most improbable that in such a car an improvised room was curtained off; if so, we should have heard a good deal about it from various people who have written about the journey.

I have in hand your letter regarding my son; I have not yet become well enough to take it up, but will do so as soon as I can.[17]

Very truly yours,
Robert T. Lincoln

16. The most recent, most authoritative attempt to untangle the puzzle of the five surviving holograph copies of the Gettysburg Address was made by David C. Mearns and Lloyd A. Dunlap in "Notes and Comments on The Preparation of the Address" in a monograph, *Long Remembered* (Washington, Library of Congress, 1963). The first copy, which the authors designate the Nicolay copy, was written in Washington before the ceremonies, although the conclusion, in pencil, may have been written at the home of David Wills at Gettysburg. This draft was in the possession of John G. Nicolay until after his death in 1901, when it passed into the hands of John Hay. In 1916 Hay's children presented this copy and the second draft to the Library of Congress. (Hay's daughter Alice was the Mrs. Wadsworth mentioned by Robert Lincoln.) The second draft, which the authors call the Hay copy, was Lincoln's first revision, and may have been written after his return to Washington. The existence of this manuscript was not publicly known until 1906. Copy number three was made by Lincoln at the request of Edward Everett to be sold at the New York Metropolitan Fair in April, 1864. It passed through private hands until 1944, when it was purchased by the Illinois State Historical Library. The fourth copy, called the Bancroft copy, was made in February, 1864, at the request of the historian George Bancroft, for reproduction in a volume of autograph facsimiles to be sold at the Baltimore Sanitary Fair. Lincoln wrote on both sides of the paper, which made the copy unsuitable for the purpose for which it was intended. The copy is now in the Cornell University Library. The last known copy, called the Bliss copy, is the one which Lincoln wrote to replace the Bancroft copy. It is now in the Lincoln Room of the White House. Mearns and Dunlap conclude that Lincoln did not write the Gettysburg Address in any of its surviving forms on the train, but they concede the possibility that he did make notes during the trip to Gettysburg. The authors conclude, pessimistically, that "the definitive story of Lincoln and the writing of the Gettysburg address has not been told, nor is it likely that it ever can be."

17. Robert T. Lincoln's son, Abraham Lincoln, known as Jack in the family, died in London on March 5, 1890, aged sixteen. Death came from blood poisoning caused by an infected carbuncle.

HILDENE, MANCHESTER, VERMONT

December 8th, 1915

Isaac Markens, Esq.
My dear Sir:

I regret that I have been unable, before now, to acknowledge several letters of yours which I will take up in order.

On November 28th: as to my knowledge of the whereabouts of the second copy of the Address made for the Baltimore Fair, I have no personal knowledge. Nicolay says, "the both sides of the paper" copy was allowed to be kept by Mr. George Bancroft and is probably now in the Lenox Library; the second copy, which was used for lithographing, was apparently considered by Nicolay as a part of the collection of original autographs collected for the Baltimore Book and the work having been done by Colonel Alexander Bliss, he kept the whole collection, and what Nicolay means by the "whole collection" is not any collection of my Father's various copies of the Address, but the collection of manuscripts got together by Colonel Bliss.

In writing about this you say that Nicolay has accounted for all the Lincoln copies; I do not think this is at all so, for on page 12 of my reprint Nicolay says, "the number he made, and for what friends, cannot now be confidently stated, though it was probably half a dozen or more," etc., so he does not pretend to account for the location of all copies.[18]

As to the color of the large paper, the pencilled half of the Gettysburg manuscript, I can add nothing of value; I remember, as Nicolay states, the habitual use by my Father of large sized paper with wide lines for long and formal documents; I have before me at this moment one or two documents of that sort written not far from the Gettysburg time. As to the color of the paper before me, I should call it white, but perhaps the paper Nicolay had before him when he wrote was a bluish-gray, for paper of this size and color for official use is well known to me; it was used by me in London in all official documents, being prescribed by the State Department to follow the official style of binding despatches in volumes;

18

I cannot at this moment recall the blue-gray color in Civil War times, but I know that it is an old kind of paper, originating probably in the Diplomatic Service of England.

As to its use by my Father at Gettysburg I, of course, know nothing, but it does not strike me as strange that he had such paper with him there and used it, or that he used a pencil; it may be true that ink was furnished him, but it does not follow that he asked for it or used it.

You ask about the original of Mr. Everett's letter; I suppose it to be in one of seven small trunks holding my Father's papers, now in a safety deposit vault; I do not think that I have ever seen it.

In regard to Mr. Nicolay, on page 12, saying of the careful revision, that it has now become the standard text and saying on page 13 that the Baltimore fac-simile has properly become the standard text, I think I have written you my idea before, which is that I see no conflict; Mr. Nicolay distinctly states on page 12 that every copy made after the revision copy, was intended to be an exact copy, and this includes of course the Baltimore copy; the first was my Father's standard; the Baltimore copy became the public standard by reason of its publication, both being exactly alike, according to Nicolay, except for some possible accidental difference.

Referring to your letter of November 27th, I am interested in seeing the two Hay manuscripts and I can do so easily without even mentioning your name; in making a social call on Mrs. Wadsworth I can introduce the subject of the Hay copy, which you call the one page copy, because its text was furnished me by Senator Blackburn last winter when I passed upon the matter of the text for the Lincoln Memorial; in talking with her and in connection with that, I can mention and propose to do so, my wonder as to what became of the ink and pencil copy. After her correspondence with you, there can be little doubt that she will say that she has it and I need not mention you, nor Miss Nicolay, nor my previous attempts to find it.

Referring to the whereabouts of the copy lithographed for use in the Autograph Leaves book, I know only from Nicolay's article, that it was owned by Colonel Bliss as a part of the manuscripts gathered by him for the book. Colonel Bliss lived in Washington and I knew him very slightly; during my winter stays there for the last five years I have not heard of him and have had no occasion to mention him; such books of reference as I have here do not give his name; he does not appear as a member in the Book of the Metropolitan Club and I am sure he would appear in it if alive; in the Book are two members named Bliss and I should not be surprised to learn in Washington that they are his sons. When in Washington this winter I shall try to remember to make some inquiries which may lead to the present location of this copy of the Address.

I have read with great care the typewritten article, "The Original Autograph Manuscript."

I do not think it is a matter of consequence, but I am not prepared to concur with your opening statement as to the Hay manuscript having been made before the day at Gettysburg; I now remember that I saw its text last winter, as I have said before, but I do not have it sufficiently in mind to form a judgment as to that; however, knowing my Father's habits pretty well, it is my belief that he would not probably present to Colonel Hay a preliminary draft of his proposed speech. Nicolay tells of the character of the work done in making a revision after the Gettysburg day; it is to my mind, more probable that several drafts of a revision were made before one was adopted, and that one of these drafts was either given to or kept (a then unimportant matter,) by Colonel Hay who was one of my Father's secretaries, with both of whom his relations were friendly and even intimate.

In the next paragraph I have made a slight typographical correction; at the bottom of the first page I have noted, what are to me, some odd figures: at the top of page two you make an argument upon the pencilled words at the bottom of the first page of the ink-pencil copy; I have noted a suggestion that the first few pencilled words were written with a short unsharpened pencil, the next page with a good one; it seems unlikely to me that the writer wrote the word, "dedicated," in two different geographical localities. At the bottom of the third page you comment upon Nicolay not mentioning the Hay all-ink copy; as indicated above, I do not think the all-ink copy was written before the Address was delivered and I think that it was not regarded as important by Nicolay, being merely a step in the revision process.

I do not understand your point in the first four lines of page three; you speak of Wilson announcing in 1913 that a copy was written in Washington and there presented to Colonel Hay, after having written that it was drafted in Washington and there presented to Hay after the trip to Gettysburg; I do not see the point of the sentence.

I never before heard of Wilson's report of an offer to Nicolay for the ink-pencil copy. Did Wilson say what Nicolay responded?

Down in the middle of page three, the story about the small sheets of paper given to Mr. Everett is rather absurd in view of Mr. Everett's letter to my Father; further on in page three it does not seem to have occurred to you that the, "Original Manuscript," exhibited at Boston by Miss Keyes, bound up with Everett's oration, if the story is true, could only be the copy presented to Mr. Everett by my Father in pursuance of Mr. Everett's request for it, in which he asks permission to bind it with his own manuscript to be given to Mrs. Fish for use (that is, to be sold,) at the Metropolitan Fair; (Nicolay's article, page 12;). You refer to it as being nothing more than one of several copies furnished to various applicants; that is of course true, but Mr. Everett should hardly, I think, be referred to as one of "various applicants."

On page four there is a misnomer as to Colonel Hay's elder daughter; she is Mrs. Payne Whitney. One of W. C. Whitney's sons is Harry Payne Whitney, who married Miss Gertrude Vanderbuilt; the other is Payne Whitney, who married Miss Helen Hay.

I have no objection to the use of my name in connection with the Memorial; I try in every way to have the Baltimore text taken as standard

I return the manuscript and trust that it will reach you safely.

Very truly yours,

Robert T. Lincoln

18. See p. 17, n. 16.

HILDENE, MANCHESTER, VERMONT

November 13th, 1916

My dear Sir:

I have been in the west for a week, delaying a few days to recover from the election.

I am very glad that you were able to assist Mr. Chandler to get back his Commission for I am sure that he will wish it to remain in his family. I was sorry to hear from a friend in Chicago that Mr. Chandler is now very feeble; if he is to be in Washington this winter I shall make a special effort to see him; he is now nearly eighty-one years of age and I fancy that it was a matter of deep regret to him that he was not able to take his usual vigorous and effective part in political work this year.[19]

Thank you very much for sending me the sale catalogue with so many Lincoln items in it; some of them of the 1860 and 1861 time are quite interesting to me, but of course I have long passed the time of wishing to add to my own collection of such things. As you may wish to retain it, I return the cutting to you.

It will give me pleasure to put my name to the two pictures of myself of which you speak if you will send them to me. I will also see if I cannot look up a later picture of myself; but not very recent, for I have none. In writing to you before, I overlooked your request for such a thing.

Very truly yours,

Robert T. Lincoln

Isaac Markens, Esq.

19. William Eaton Chandler, a power in the Republican Party, served as Secretary of the Navy in Chester A. Arthur's cabinet, and as United States Senator from New Hampshire from 1887 to 1901. He died in 1917.

HILDENE, MANCHESTER, VERMONT

November 17th, 1916

My dear Sir:

Replying to your note enclosing two small photographs of myself and one of each of my brothers, William and Thomas, I have as you request indicated the dates of the birth and death of my brothers.[20] As to the two pictures of myself, I have signed one of them, but am taking the liberty of retaining the other for the reason that it is a photograph of myself which I have never liked and trusted was out of existence. It was taken about the time of my recovery from an illness and may be properly described as a "sick looking" picture. Instead of it I am sending you a photograph taken perhaps a little later than that. Lastly, I am sending you one of the last photographs taken of me; I think it is about ten years old.

I trust that this will be satisfactory to you.

Very truly yours,

Robert T. Lincoln

Isaac Markens, Esq.

20. William Wallace Lincoln, December 21, 1850 – February 20, 1862, and Thomas Lincoln, April 4, 1853 – July 15, 1871.

HILDENE, MANCHESTER, VERMONT

November 17th, 1916

My dear Sir:

Since writing my previous letter of this date, I notice in the last number of the Harvard Bulletin, at page 144, in the announcement of the presentation by Mrs. Rothschild of her husband's library to Harvard, that his posthumous work is announced for publication in the spring under the title, "Honest Abe." I am sorry that such a title has been adopted; from my impression of Mr. Rothschild's dignity of style, gained from his former book on Lincoln, I could not have thought such a title would meet his approval if suggested to him.[21] There is no doubt that such a designation at one time was used by some newspaper writers; I do not know who invented it, but I have an impression that in the catalogue of Autograph sales which you sent me, its invention was claimed by Joe Medill.[22] I do not know whether it will surprise you to know that after his youth at least, my father was never addressed familiarly and personally by anything but his last name, even by his most intimate friends. It seems to me that the use in the way proposed of this temporary and not very widely extended vulgarity is unbecoming the dignity which I trust will characterize, as it has before done, Mr. Rothschild's work.

Very truly yours,
Robert T. Lincoln

Isaac Markens, Esq.

21. In 1906 Alonzo Rothschild, a New York author, published *Lincoln, Master of Men: A Study in Character* (Houghton Mifflin, Boston and New York). Rothschild died in 1915, with a second Lincoln book in manuscript.

22. Joseph Medill was part-owner, and later editor, of the *Chicago Tribune* from 1853 until his death in 1899. The term, "Honest Abe," was applied to Lincoln when he lived at New Salem, but Medill and his associates on the *Tribune* gave it wide currency in their reports of the Lincoln-Douglas debates and the presidential campaign of 1860.

HILDENE, MANCHESTER, VERMONT

November 19th, 1916

My dear Sir:

I am much gratified by your note of yesterday in regard to the title of Mr. Rothschild's forthcoming book. As I said to you, my information is derived from the Harvard Alumni Bulletin, dated November 16th, which I received day before yesterday. At page 144 there is a short but interesting article headed, The Lincoln Collection, being the library of Mr. Rothschild given to Harvard University by Mrs. Rothschild. A paragraph reads as follows:

"His study of Lincoln won him wide recognition. A second volume, dealing with Lincoln's earlier career, was nearly ready for publication at the time of Mr. Rothschild's death. This has been completed, and is announced for publication in the spring, under the title, 'Honest Abe.' "

This is the only announcement of publication which has come to my attention. In writing to you it did not occur to me that the title might be settled by the publisher. As you say that the Houghton Mifflin Company settled the title of the first book, if the same publisher has the new book perhaps it is not too late for me to take up the matter myself if necessary. Mr. George Mifflin was in the next class to me at Harvard and I have known him well for more than fifty years, and I would not hesitate to write him on the subject, being certain that my letter would receive every possible attention. In the New York Times Book Review, dated yesterday, but which we receive with the Sunday Times of today, the Houghton Mifflin Company's announcement of new books does not include the one in question; nor is it mentioned in the notice on the last page of the Review which, however, refers to the books listed in it as having been just published. Perhaps Houghton Mifflin Company is not the publisher.

Awaiting a note from you on this matter with great interest,

Very truly yours,

Robert T. Lincoln

Isaac Markens, Esq.

HILDENE, MANCHESTER, VERMONT

November 21st, 1916

My dear Sir:

I am glad to have your note of yesterday and return to you the two letters enclosed in it. Your suggestion as to the possible origin of the alleged title is quite possible. I infer that you have already written to the Houghton Mifflin Company; if it turns out that the adoption of a title depends upon Houghton Mifflin Company and you find any difficulty in the matter, I think that it is better that I should take it up with Mr. Mifflin who, as I have intimated to you, is an old, personal friend of mine and whatever I said to him on the subject would be as confidential as I should myself desire.

I do not recall the letter of my mother written in 1861 of which you speak. She was a voluminous writer and I am rather afraid that the making of a copy of it would be a good deal of trouble; if, however, it is short I should be greatly obliged for a copy.

Very truly yours,
Robert T. Lincoln

Isaac Markens, Esq.

HILDENE, MANCHESTER, VERMONT

November 22nd, 1916

My dear Sir:

Of course I am as you are, very much disappointed by the note of Mrs. Rothschild which I return to you.

I am writing to Mr. George Mifflin today a letter telling him the substance of Mrs. Rothschild's note and I have ventured to quote your feeling that the choice was a tentative preference, etc. I trust that you will not object to this.

I appreciate greatly the trouble you have taken in this matter. I shall of course let you know anything further that comes to me.

Very truly yours,
Robert T. Lincoln

Isaac Markens, Esq.

HILDENE, MANCHESTER, VERMONT

November 24th, 1916

My dear Sir:

I return to you the Houghton Mifflin Company letter. What he says about Mr. Rothschild is curious; no doubt my father was honest, but so are most men. The fact is that the epithet was the outcome of a state of civilization which did not know how to express itself with propriety. At the same period in which Medill invented this there was a wild hurrah in the State Convention when two or three fence rails, said to be a part of a lot which my father had assisted in making, were brought in; those doing it probably thought that they were the best argument for his ensuing nomination as a candidate for the United States Senate. The incident, as you know, caused him to be widely spoken of as "the rail splitter."[23] Perhaps the Houghton Mifflin Company letter means to indicate that this latter subtitle will be added to the former one.

I thank you very much for the copy of the alleged letter of my mother; frankly I do not believe it to be genuine; it is not at all like her style and you will observe that it is dated June 20th, and in its rather florid language states "on every field the prowess of Kentuckians has been manifested." I am not taking the trouble to examine to see just what possible fighting occurred after the fall of Fort Sumter, April 14th, 1861, but I am quite sure there was nothing of any consequence until the first battle of Bull Run, which took place July 21st, 1861, more than a month after the date of the alleged letter.

Another thing strikes me. Your copy indicates that this was published in the Petersburg Express, July 29th, 1861; at the end of the letter occur the words, "our common country"; I have not time at the moment to look this up, but I think that the phrase "our common country," was invented a long time after that date by my father. I do not recall any use of it before 1865 when Jefferson Davis wrote a letter to F.P.Blair, Sr., in regard to a conference in which he used the expression, "with a view to securing peace to "the two countries." Mr. Blair showed that letter to my father, who thereupon wrote to Mr. Blair on January 18th, 1865, referring to it and expressing his readiness to receive an agent who might be sent by Mr. Davis "with the view of securing peace to the people of our one common country."

The two letters were of course in effect a correspondence between Mr. Davis and President Lincoln and the expression of the latter was a retort to the former; perhaps the phrase had been used before somewhere, but I do not recall it.

Very truly yours,
Robert T. Lincoln

Isaac Markens, Esq.

23. The incident took place in the Illinois State Republican Convention, held at Decatur on May 9, 1860, rather than in 1858, when Lincoln was a candidate for the United States Senate.

HILDENE, MANCHESTER, VERMONT

November 30th, 1916

Dear Mr. Markens:

Your letter of the 26th came to me a day or two ago, but I delayed writing you thinking I might hear again from Mr. Mifflin. It seems that I had not told you that I wrote to Mr. Mifflin and received a reply of the most friendly character, not expressing his own opinion on the title, but indicating the obsession of Mrs. Rothschild. Mr. Mifflin went so far as to say that he would not publish this book with a title which was offensive to me on my serious consideration of it. I replied to him expressing my appreciation, but suggesting that it was really up to the lady; if she insisted on the title and if Mr. Mifflin thereupon threw up the publication on my account, it would simply mean that she would procure another publisher and as I said to him, the matter would end with no satisfaction to either of us, and that I hoped that the result would be that she could be persuaded to change the title. I have not since heard from him.

You are right about the "Honest Abe" epithet. I of course read Dr. Holland's book when it came out in 1866; I do not think I had looked in it since then and I had entirely forgotten this particular thing.[24] I wrote another letter to Mr. Mifflin, telling him that I was wrong about Medill having invented the expression, but indicating that I did not think that that made much difference, and that I did not think a serious book about Lincoln ought to have as a title a soubriquet given him when twenty-two years old by the small gang in which he moved at the time, who must have felt themselves a hard lot by indicating that he was the only honest man among them. So there we are.

I return to you the two letters you enclosed. Dr. Wayland's letter I say nothing about; I think he is right from his very evident point of view. I should have expected something better from President White; it may be that at his age he gave no serious consideration to your question.[25]

Your views about the supposed letter of my mother are interesting and perhaps you are right in your explanation.

I had not seen the Herndon item in the Times of the 26th inst., but have looked it up and when I get to Washington I may drop you a line on the subject. I am at this moment very busy in getting ready to leave here this evening for Washington for the winter.

Very truly yours,
Robert T. Lincoln

Isaac Markens, Esq.

24. J. G. Holland, in his *Life of Abraham Lincoln* (Springfield, Mass., 1866), had asserted that Lincoln had acquired the sobriquet of "Honest Abe" while clerking in Denton Offut's store in New Salem.

25. The allusion to the letters of Dr. Wayland and President White remains a mystery to the editor. President White was undoubtedly Andrew Dickson White, president of Cornell University from 1867 to 1885, diplomat, and author.

1775 N STREET, WASHINGTON, D.C.

December 6th, 1916

My dear Mr. Markens:

I got here on the first inst. and have been as busy as my health permits me to be. I have had several notes from you which I have not acknowledged for the reason that in consequence of a note from Mr. Greenslet of the Houghton, Mifflin Company,[26] received just as I left Manchester, I thought it possible that he himself might call upon me here on any day.

The opinions you have been at the trouble to procure do not of course help our campaign much, if there was any possible help for it. I see clearly by Mr. Greenslet's letter of last week, which has the endorsement of Mr. Mifflin, that the situation is to be as I suspected in a former letter; Mrs. Rothschild is obsessed by her sacred duty and if Mr. Mifflin should refuse to use the title over my objection, she would demand permission to go to another publisher. That is a result that would do us no good and naturally I do not wish uselessly to interfere in the Houghton, Mifflin business.

I am trying to think the matter out as to a sub-title as to which there might not be the same difficulty of dealing with Mrs. Rothschild. I have come to no satisfactory conclusion in my own mind, but the line on which I am thinking is this: Doctor Holland indicates that the soubriquet was acquired at a date when my father was 21 or 22 years of age and in a small and rude community; this community had no idea of the characteristic being based not only upon the simple qualities of pecuniary honesty and truth telling, but upon the qualities exhibited in the 20 years following in a career which had broadened out into a legal, professional life and a political life. Mr. Rothschild's book, which ends as you say upon my father's election to Congress, is based of course upon the whole of that early part of his life and therefore the use of the word "honest," which might well be applied to the youngest office boy, is not broad enough, in fact, for what Mr. Rothschild wished it to be; the question in my mind is how can it be broadened by a better sub-title. That is as far as I have got at present.

Sincerely yours,

Robert T. Lincoln

Isaac Markens, Esq.

26. Ferris Greenslet, general manager and editor in chief of the Houghton Mifflin Company, 1910 to 1942.

1775 N STREET, WASHINGTON, D.C.

December 10th, 1916

Dear Mr. Markens:

I return the letter in regard to Captain Fry, which you sent me in connection with the letter of my mother; I do not think I ever before heard of him.[27] Perhaps my father had more to do with the writing and fulness of the letter than I imagined; he was especially interested as to the attitude of Kentucky in the beginning of the war; for example, the husband of one of my mother's half-sisters, who is now the sole survivor of her father's family,[28] was then the young wife of Ben Hardin Helm, a brilliant young lawyer of Kentucky who had graduated from West Point and resigned from the army to go into civil life. My father earnestly desired to give him a commission in the Federal Army, but he refused to sever his relations with those of his friends who were going into the Confederate Army and he became commander of a noted confederate organization called the Orphan's Brigade and was killed at Chickamauga.

I duly received your note of suggestions for the book title, dated December 7th; as you know, on the day I received it Mr. Greenslet was here and saw it. I have a letter from him this morning telling me of his conversation with you yesterday; he says that the discussion narrowed down to three possibilities which he enclosed; the first one has the sub-title, The Making of a President. For this he expresses the preference and at this moment I agree with him, but I still think there is a chance of improvement, over which I am pondering and may give you the result in a P.S. to this.

My ideas are now running as follows: I think a short sub-title is far better because it would accord with the sub-title of the other book; I also would be glad to have it so short that it might be printed on the back edge of the book. At the present moment I have not the Lincoln Master of Men book before me, but it seems to me that I am right in thinking that as the book stands in a shelf it reads,

Lincoln
Master of
Men.

I am particularly desirous to have a title so short that it will be seen on the back edge of the book and used as completely as his Lincoln Master of Men. This thought occurs to me,

Honest Abe
President
In Making.

or

Honest Abe
The
President
In Making.

Well, I am afraid I am at the end. I think The Making of a President is the best sub-title, if it can be made to go on the back edge of the book; if not I would personally prefer one of my two suggestions just above this.

However, I am writing to Mr. Greenslet in substance as I am writing to you above; there I feel I must leave it so far as I am concerned. I appreciate very much the great interest and help you have given in this matter. You will of course understand that I still do not like the "Honest

Abe" business at all, but I am acting on the understanding that there is no escape from that part of it.

Sincerely yours,

Robert T. Lincoln

Isaac Markens, Esq.

27. In early June, 1861, John Fry of Boyle County, Kentucky, applied to Lincoln for a pair of Navy revolvers and a sabre. Fry expected to raise and command a company of Union troops, and said it was impossible for him to procure the accoutrements he needed. Lincoln sent Fry's letter to the Secretary of War with an endorsement, dated June 17, 1861: "I will thank the Secretary of War, if he will have us furnished, the 'Navy-revolvers and Sabre' as desired within, so that Mrs. L. can send them with her compliments. Mr. Fry is an acquaintance of hers, and a good & brave man." *Collected Works of Abraham Lincoln*, IV, 410.

28. Emily Helm, eighteen years younger than her half-sister. After Ben Hardin Helm's death the Lincolns took his widow into the White House, an act of mercy and solicitude which brought considerable criticism upon them.

1775 N STREET, WASHINGTON, D.C.

December 20th, 1916

Dear Mr. Markens:

I have your note of yesterday and return to you the letter of Miss Tarbell.[29] My failure to do so at once, as I did with others you have sent me, was accidental.

As you have learned, Mrs. Rothschild has issued her ultimatum which of course under the circumstances ends the business, and while I have not yet acknowledged Mr. Greenslet's letter, he of course understands that the subject is closed, as in my last letter to him I said, "I therefore must leave the whole matter with you." I have no dissatisfaction with Mr. Greenslet; on the contrary I am greatly obliged to him; I am sure he has done all he could to meet our views. He could not get rid of the "Honest Abe" title and with that at the top my dissatisfaction will be felt whenever I may happen to recall the existence of the book.[30]

I renew the assurance of my great appreciation of the trouble you have taken in the matter.

Very sincerely yours,
Robert T. Lincoln

Isaac Markens, Esq.

29. Ida M. Tarbell, journalist, author of *The Early Life of Abraham Lincoln* (1896), *Life of Abraham Lincoln* (1900), and other important works on nineteenth and early twentieth century American historical subjects.

30. *"Honest Abe"* was published with the subtitle, *A Study in Integrity based on the Early Life of Abraham Lincoln*, by the Houghton Mifflin Company, 1917.

1775 N STREET, WASHINGTON, D.C.

January 5th, 1917

Dear Mr. Markens:

Your letter of December 28th, was duly received, but has been laid aside in the pressure of this time of the year.

Mr. Greenslet of course wrote me a final letter to which I replied, throwing up the sponge.

In regard to the Bixby letter there is a mystery which I have been unable to solve and into which I cannot go now because my correspondence relating to it is in my files in Manchester and inaccessible to me until next spring. Briefly I can say that unfortunately I did not take up the question as to the existence or location of the original Bixby letter until after the death of Mr. Nicolay; it was he and not Colonel Hay who did the work of compiling the two final documentary volumes of their Biography.[31] Colonel Hay died about ten years ago and before that I had received from the Republican Club of New York, a package of lithographed Lincoln letters which the Club had got up as a present to their guests at one of their Annual Lincoln Birthday Dinners; among these lithographs was that of the Bixby letter. I was a very busy man in those days, but on one of my visits in New York I made an effort to ascertain the location of the document from which the lithograph was made. As I remember I found that the Republican Club was not a social club having a house and a standing financial and clerical organization such as the ordinary large social club, for example, as the Union Club of New York has. I finally secured an interview with one or two gentlemen of the Club who were on the dinner committee for that particular dinner; neither of them could then tell me anything about the getting up of these particular souvenirs, but they promised that they would investigate the matter and communicate with me again; they never did so and in the pressure of my other affairs, this went out of my mind. Then there came to me from a man named Benson a curious letter which had some queer things about it which led me in acknowledging it not to use my own name, but to have my Secretary, Mr. Sweet, now dead, act for me. As I remember, Benson said that he owned the original Bixby letter and that it was pledged for a loan on $100, I think, made to him by a Brooklyn banker, and that it was his intention to present it to me. Sweet wrote him suggesting that he cause the letter to be sent to any bank in Chicago for me to inspect and that if I considered it genuine I would be very glad to pay his debt to the Brooklyn banker instead of having him give me the letter. I think Benson then replied that it was not possible for him to go to Brooklyn to arrange this for some time to come, but that in the meantime he being hard up, would like to have me cash a note of his for an amount which I now forget, but I think it was $250; this he enclosed to avoid delay and it was returned to him. I cannot remember other details, but being in Washington I showed Colonel Hay, in the State Department, this lithograph and told him the story; Colonel Hay knew nothing whatever of the source of the printed copy of the letter in the Nicolay and Hay book. He suggested a curious thing; namely, that my father's hand writing was very easy to imitate. This I knew myself because several times as a boy to amuse myself I used to write his ordinary signature so well that I think it would have passed muster with himself. Colonel Hay went on to say that pretty nearly all the words in the Bixby letter could be found in photographs of genuine letters and that perhaps this lithograph had been made from a forged document. I think Colonel Hay's suggestion a very shrewd one.

I examined the Museum document as well as I could, it being

framed in a case, and I came to the conclusion that it was simply one of the facsimile copies of the lithograph. You speak of some facsimile copies differing from others in the signature; my copy is in Manchester and I cannot recall whether the signature is in full or not. That is the end of my investigation. I do not remember having brought to my attention any other supposed lithograph of the letter; there may be things in my files additional to what I have written and if you will call my attention to the matter next summer I will again look it up.

Both Mr. Sweet and myself were strongly impressed with the feeling that Mr. Benson was not a gentleman with whom we would care to do business. Very curiously some years after that Sweet told me that Benson was on the roll of the White House as doorkeeper or messenger; otherwise I have entirely lost track of him.

When I speak of the possible forgery I do not of course mean that there was not a genuine Bixby letter; I mean merely that a shrewd forger could from the printed copy in the Nicolay and Hay book, make an apparently genuine original. Personally I have no doubt of the authenticity of the letter, but who Mrs. Bixby was and what was her local address and where the original letter is, I have not the slightest idea.[32]

Sincerely yours,

Robert T. Lincoln

Isaac Markens, Esq.

31. *Abraham Lincoln. Complete Works, Comprising his Speeches, Letters, State Papers, and Miscellaneous Writings.* Edited by John G. Nicolay and John Hay. 2 vols., New York, 1894.

32. It has long been established that the facsimiles of the Bixby letter are reproductions of forgeries. The original letter, though reputed to exist in many places, has never come to light. But Robert Lincoln was right about the authenticity of the letter: of that there can be no doubt. Mrs. Lydia Bixby, a widow, had five sons in the Union army, but her case had been inaccurately presented to Lincoln. Two were killed. One was captured, and either went over to the Confederacy or died in prison: his fate remains unknown. A fourth son was honorably discharged after having served for the term of his enlistment. The fifth son deserted.

1775 N STREET, WASHINGTON, D.C.

February 19th, 1917

Dear Mr. Markens:

I duly received your letter of the 15th inst. Your citation as to the Edwin Booth story is slightly in error. I found it in Volume 55, New Series, of the Century, at page 920, being in the April number, 1902. The quotation there shown as in a letter from me is exactly correct, for I remember writing it; I cannot here tell to whom the letter was written, but it exactly states the incident as it occurred.[33]

I am much interested in the new information you give me about Mrs. Bixby. I supposed that my old Secretary, Mr. Sweet, had exhausted the possibilities of the case, but it seems not; I shall now endeavor to find here the report of the Adjutant General of Massachusetts to which you refer. As to the signature, I may be incorrect in saying that my lithograph is simply A. Lincoln and my idea may really be guesswork from knowing that my father almost never wrote his full name except in signing formal documents. I shall be much interested as to the result of your further research as to the origin of Tobin's lithograph; he may be the man who made the lithographs for the dinner of the Republican Club of New York, from which my copy came.[34]

Very truly yours,

Robert T. Lincoln

Isaac Markens, Esq.

33. The Chicago Historical Society recently acquired an original letter, written May 6, 1919, by Robert T. Lincoln, containing his account of the Edwin Booth episode. The letter reads in part as follows:

"In 1863 or 1864 I started from New York to Washington taking at Jersey City a midnight train standing in the station, having a sleeping car. The stone platform was level with the car platform on which stood a conductor selling berth tickets to a line of passengers who stood leaning against the side of the car. The line made quite a little crowd of which I was one. Suddenly the train began to move & by the motion & the crowding of my neighbors, I was screwed off my feet, which dropped down into the slot between the car & the platform—not very far but the situation was very dangerous. A man seized my collar & jerked me with great vigor out of the slot and onto my feet, on the platform. Moving to thank him I easily recognized Edwin Booth, having often seen him on the stage. I think that he later learned my name from a friend of his, who was a fellow-staff officer of mine, to whom I related the incident at City Point, in 1865."

The statement bears the name of no addressee, but was undoubtedly written to Mrs. Ben Hardin Helm (Emily Todd).

34. Michael F. Tobin, a New York dealer in pictures and prints, copyrighted an engraving of the Bixby letter in 1891, and began selling copies in that same year. No one knows who "created" the manuscript from which reproductions were made. William E. Barton, *A Beautiful Blunder: The True Story of Lincoln's Letter to Mrs. Lydia A. Bixby* (Indianapolis, 1926), pp. 50–54.

1775 N STREET, WASHINGTON, D.C.

February 24th, 1917

Dear Mr. Markens:

I think I have not acknowledged your letter of February 20th, in regard to the Bixby letter. Your suggestion that neither Nicolay nor Hay probably had any special knowledge of the letter at the time is correct. Hay himself told me so;[35] when I took the matter up Nicolay had died and it was he who had compiled the collection of papers. It is entirely possible that neither of them knew of the letter at all; my father had no letter books and copies of his letters and documents were only made in special cases, many such copies being in the papers I now have; mostly drafts in his own hand—it is entirely possible that my father wrote this letter at his desk, folded it, addressed it and gave it to General Schouler without anybody else about him knowing of it.

I have Benson's letters, but they are in my files at Manchester where my house is absolutely closed and it is impracticable to get at the package containing the Benson letters. I will do so upon my return there in the spring, but I doubt whether he is of any consequence in the business; he perhaps intended to try to impose something upon me, but whether or not that is true, he acted in such a way as to make me very suspicious of him and I lost interest in him. I will however look the matter up on my return to Vermont.

Mr. Morrison, of the Library of Congress, has been good enough to send me a phototype copy of a Boston newspaper article giving a reduced lithograph of the letter and photograph of Mrs. Bixby's residence and a very elaborate account of the Bixby family, all of which is quite interesting to have in my papers and I am indebted to you for putting me in the way of getting it.

I have this morning your letter of yesterday about the Cadman speech and your supplementary note. I strongly suspect that what Mr. Cadman has, is merely one of the lithographic copies, but it may turn out differently.

The torn and soiled paper spoken of as having been found in rubbish near the New York post-office may safely, I fancy, be guessed to be one of the lithograph letters which undoubtedly became very numerous.

I am afraid with you that further search in this matter is useless.

Very sincerely yours,
Robert T. Lincoln

Isaac Markens, Esq.

35. This statement should dispose of the allegation that John Hay, because of his literary felicity, must have written the Bixby letter. Those who have read this far in this book will have been impressed with the accuracy of Robert Lincoln's recollections.

HILDENE, MANCHESTER, VERMONT

August 15, 1917

Dear Mr. Markens:

I have your note of the 13th, and am a little surprised that the Rothschild book has not yet been published. I have been very much out of health during the whole winter, and am still, but I had a vague idea that the book had already been published, and was rejoicing that interest in it had been overwhelmed by the general condition of public affairs.

I am afraid that I can give you no information whatever in regard to your questions. I do not at this moment know where my father's supposed statement about the influence of his mother is to be found. I think it very likely that the statement is one of the many inventions regarding him. It is my memory that the expression given was "angel mother." I know that my father had a great affection for his stepmother, but it is unlikely that he would have referred to her as his "angel mother," because she survived him, and the use of the word "angel" in the way it is purported to have been used, would, it seems to me, have been unlikely.[36]

I know nothing whatever in regard to the last photograph of my father. Perhaps Mr. Frederick Hill Meserve, #949 Madison Avenue, New York City, who has given more attention than anyone else to the collection of Lincoln photographs could answer your question.

In regard to the Hampton Roads conference story, I am equally at a loss. Of course you have seen my father's own official account of it, which is printed at page 138, Volume X, of Nicolay and Hay's Work, in which nothing of the sort appears. In the case of a man who was as careful as my father was it seems to me most unlikely that on such an occasion he would have used the language imputed to him, as to accepting any terms proposed if only the restoration of the Union was the dominating one. I do not recall where the story originated, nor can I recall where the other story originated, in which it was said that one of the Commissioners suggested that he could find a precedent for action upon one of their requests in the history of Charles 1st; he is said to have replied to this that he thought Mr. Seward was more competent on historical questions than he was, and that he only remembered most distinctly about Charles 1st that he lost his head. It was at least a very good story, but may or may not be true.

Sincerely yours,

Robert T. Lincoln

Isaac Markens, Esquire
New York City

36. The story appeared first in *Herndon's Lincoln* (1889 ed.), I, pp. 3–4. But Herndon had quoted Lincoln as having said: "God bless my mother; all that I am or ever hope to be I owe to her."

HILDENE, MANCHESTER, VERMONT

Isaac Markens, Esq.
    545 West 164th Street
    New York City
Dear Mr. Markens:

I am very glad to have your note of the 26th in regard to the New York Sun article on the Barnard statue;[37] you do not mention the New York Times Editorial article of the same date, August 26th, which is also very gratifying to me.[38]

I must differ from you in respect to the statue. I think it simply horrible. I am having printed here some items which will interest you and which I will send as soon as the printer gives them to me, which may be a few days, as the office is small and at the moment it is busy in getting out the weekly edition of its newspaper.

I make no concealment of the fact that I am doing what I think is possible to prevent this thing from being set up either in London or Paris.[39]

Sincerely yours,
Robert T. Lincoln

37. In 1910 Charles P. Taft, half-brother of William Howard Taft, and Mrs. Charles P. Taft gave $100,000 for the creation of a statue of Lincoln to be erected in Cincinnati, the Taft home. The commission was awarded to George Grey Barnard, an eminent sculptor. The statue, unveiled on March 31, 1917, immediately aroused violent controversy.

38. The editorial was inspired by pictures of the Barnard statue in *The Art World* and was headed, "Is Lincoln a Slump?" The writer granted Barnard's well-earned reputation, but believed that in this statue he was "governed by a perverse spirit. . . . Barnard's Lincoln is not only plain, but grotesque. We doubt the accuracy of the portrait." The editor contrasted Lincoln's vitality, dignity, and strength with the posture of the statue. "Barnard's Lincoln, on the other hand, is a long suffering peasant crushed by adversity. His pose is ungainly, the figure lacks dignity, and the huge hands crossed over the stomach suggest that all is not well with his digestion. The largeness of the hands is unduly exaggerated."

39. At the time, movements were on foot to place replicas of the Barnard statue in London and Paris.

HILDENE, MANCHESTER, VERMONT

September 7, 1917

Dear Mr. Markens:

I have your note of August 29th, and am now enclosing some of the printed material which I am using in my effort to prevent the setting up in London and in Paris of the statue of my father by Mr. Barnard.[40] I cannot agree with you in your remark that the whole question turns on one's choice or dislike of the period of its representation. As I said in my letter to Mr. Taft, it is grotesque as a likeness of my father at any time. I prefer to deal with the statue as a whole without myself attempting to add to the list of absurdities mentioned in The Art World,[41] but to you I will say that I could add a word on the matter of the feet. It happens that I remember my father perfectly from the time when he was a member of Congress. His footgear and that of people like him at that time was boots, and it happens that he was very particular about his boots. In my knowledge of him he never owned a pair of shoes, and the representation by Barnard in that respect and in the general deformity (I do not mean size) [is] as grotesquely absurd for my father as it would be for any of his associates.

Please look at Figure 12 on page 212 of The Art World for June. I do not ask your opinion but for myself I cannot help having the feeling that the man who as a sculptor made the feet of which that photograph is a representation, might be suspected of having a "screw loose."

Very sincerely yours,

Robert T. Lincoln

Isaac Markens, Esq.
New York, N.Y.

40. A persistent effort has failed to turn up a single copy of the "printed material" referred to here.

41. Among the "absurdities" mentioned in an article entitled, "A Mistake in Bronze," which appeared in *The Art World* for June, 1917, were Barnard's concept of

Lincoln's "slouchiness," the artist's depiction of the President in nondescript clothing ("Lincoln always dressed in the best clothes his money could buy"), and the "clumsy and lumpy feet, utterly untrue to Lincoln." In a letter to his aunt, Mrs. Ben Hardin Helm, November 29, 1917, Robert T. Lincoln called the copies of the Barnard statue to be sent to Europe "two horrible monsters."

HILDENE, MANCHESTER, VERMONT

September 14, 1917

My dear Mr. Markens:

Excuse me for my delay in acknowledging your note of October 9th which I have read with interest, but I have been very much occupied.

I have, of course, seen Mr. Taft's speech at Cincinnati, and I do not intend to attempt to prevail upon him to withdraw his expressions. I suppose "Henry Gurley" whom you mention is Harrison Gourley, who as a boy lived in Springfield in his father's house, the rear line of whose lot was separated from the rear line of our lot by the usual block alley. In that way he, of course, often saw my father, but I should be surprised to know that he ever heard him as a speaker.

I have long known of the Committee whose names are published in regard to the statue for Paris. I saw a letter addressed to one gentleman by Barnard, inviting him to become a member of that Committee to present a statue of Lincoln to Paris.[42] He knew nothing of the statue, but was inclined to assent to the invitation as a mark of respect to my father, which he was carefully advised would cost him no money, but he happened to meet me, and promptly declined. I do not know how many of those whose names were printed were in a similar condition of ignorance, for I am not bothering about that part of the business. In the New York Sun of August 12th, I see a statement was issued by the Committee in which they described themselves as "America." This seems to me rather a large assumption of magnitude. You ask whether I have seen the statue. I am glad to tell you that I have never seen the beastly thing and I hope I may never do so. I am quite satisfied that the photographs I have seen do not lie in depicting its various atrocities. Photographs could not show them if they did not exist.

Very sincerely yours,

Robert T. Lincoln

42. The Paris project never materialized, but a replica was placed in Manchester, England, in 1919, and another in Louisville, Kentucky, in 1922.

HILDENE, MANCHESTER, VERMONT

October 2, 1917

Isaac Markens, Esq.
　New York, New York
Dear Mr. Markens:

I have your letter of September 30th in regard to Mr. Barnard's fourteen feet high head of my father, in which you say I would like it.[43] I am quite confident that I would not like it for several reasons, two of which at least are that I do not see how I could take any interest in a head of anybody fourteen feet high, except in wondering what can be the use of the creation of such a monstrosity. There is, of course, no use in my going over again my other objections to Mr. Barnard's work. As he says himself, it was based upon a rejection of all photographs, of which there are scores, as you know. The only fact upon which he acted, according to himself, was the personal appearance of the tall splitter of rails born near Hodgenville, Kentucky.[44] I must therefore frankly say to you that I would not care to see the photograph you speak of.

I have had on my desk unacknowledged the pamphlet entitled "The Hampton Roads Conference," by Mr. Carr. I have read this with great interest and closeness, and in spite of the insistence of my dear old friend Colonel Watterson,[45] I think that Mr. Carr comes to the correct conclusion upon consideration of such facts as he mentions, which are probably

44

all that can be had, that the story of the blank page with "Union" at the top is a fiction. I am very glad to have the pamphlet, and thank you for it.[46]

Very sincerely yours,
Robert T. Lincoln

43. Markens had written that he had just visited Barnard's studio and had admired his gigantic head of Lincoln. Rashly, Markens told Robert T. Lincoln, "I know you will like it," and asked permission to send a photograph which the sculptor had given him.

44. Barnard had taken for his model a Kentuckian of the same height and general build as the President.

45. Henry Watterson, editor of the *Louisville Courier-Journal*.

46. In 1917 Julian S. Carr, president of the Bull Durham Tobacco Company, Durham, North Carolina, published a pamphlet entitled *The Hampton Roads Conference: A Refutation of the Statement that Mr. Lincoln said if Union was written at the top the Southern Commissioners might fill in the balance.*

The Hampton Roads Conference, held February 3, 1865, was an attempt to bring the Civil War to a close. Lincoln and William H. Seward represented the Union; Alexander H. Stephens, R. M. T. Hunter, and J. A. Campbell the Confederacy. The conference accomplished nothing.

HILDENE, MANCHESTER, VERMONT

October 17, 1917

My dear Mr. Markens:

I thank you for your letter of yesterday enclosing articles from the Sun, which it happens I have also seen, as I read the Sun and Times steadily. I am glad to feel that the interest in this business is growing in the direction which I wish.

I am glad also to have your criticism of Mr. Rothschild's book, and I confess it surprises me that the man who wrote the former book should have been content to do as he has done. It is not my present expectation to read the book.

Very sincerely yours,
Robert T. Lincoln

Isaac Markens, Esq.
New York, N.Y.

HILDENE, MANCHESTER, VERMONT

October 27, 1917

My dear Mr. Markens:

Your note of the 24th reaches me only this morning. I did not examine the Lincoln portrait in last Sunday's Times very carefully, but it struck me generally as being a fairly good picture. As to the date of it, I somewhat doubt its correctness, as you do. That was the day on the morning of which he arrived in Washington so unexpectedly. It may be true, but I doubt it, that he had his photograph taken that day. I am glad to have your further opinion of the "Honest Abe" book. I have not seen it, and as I have said before, it is not my intention to do so. I have not seen the Nation or the Outlook. They are neither of them papers that I like on any account, and I should expect in them articles that would unduly disturb my equanimity.

Sincerely yours,
Robert T. Lincoln

HILDENE, MANCHESTER, VERMONT

November 4, 1917

Dear Mr. Markens:

I have many times seen newspaper squibs attributing the saying about "fooling the people, &c.",[47] to my father, but I have never given the matter any attention, and personally have no impression as to whether he ever said it or not. If William Pitt Kellogg wrote it,[48] I should think there would be little doubt that my father used the expression in his presence, but whether as a quotation or as an original remark is another matter. On the question of my father's library, there is not much to be said. Springfield, when he lived there, was not a large place, but it was the Capital, and there was for a time a very good miscellaneous library, a part of the office of the Secretary of State. I do not think there was then any private library worth speaking of in the Town. The State Library I speak of was a good room, well furnished, and was used for meeting purposes by the friends of the Secretary of State, for the time being, quite as a social club. As a fact, it was in that way that my father met Mr. Nicolay, who was the Chief Clerk and played a good game of chess, which my father liked very much, and they played many games in the Library in times of leisure. My father, of course, had some books at home. I remember well a large bookcase full of them. He had, of course, a few law books. As to them you would have to write to the ghost of Bill Herndon. I suppose he sold them. As to the private books, I do not know just how they were handled when my father left Springfield. After my mother's death, when I rounded up such things as well as I could, I found myself in possession of twenty odd books, which I now have. I will not attempt to give a catalogue of them, but among them is a set of the old Encyclopaedia Americana, and a book called "Lives of the Signers," which I have no doubt my father used in preparing his Cooper Institute speech. There is also a Milton and a few religious and philosophical works, one of them is Bunyan's Pilgrims Progress, my early interest in which I well remember. While I know the Waverly Novels made a part of the collection (there was no other fiction) I have not found those volumes, nor have I found what I would very much like to find, the old copy of Playfield's Euclid, which I recall seeing him studying in my early boyhood. There was also a large book I remember very well which I cannot find, called "Evidences of Christianity," of which the author was Dr. James Smith, our pastor, a very close friend of my father's, who died as Consul at Dundee. He was a Scotchman born, and very fond of his boyhood memories. I do not remember how I heard it, but I know it is true that immediately after the election of 1858 in Illinois, Dr. Smith was endeavoring to console my father over the result by saying, "You are beaten for the Senatorship, but the work you have done will make you President," to which my father replied, "If I am President, I will make you Consul at Dundee," and this is what he did. For a number of years after my father's death, it was my self imposed duty upon the incoming of a new Administration to make an earnest request for the retention in his office of Dr. Smith, and I never failed while he lived to have the immediate reply that he was not to be removed.

Shakespeare, of course, he always had by him, but I do not have the Shakespeare he used in Springfield. All this is not for publication, of course.

I may tell you a thing which I think is odd: I know of no book in which my father wrote his name as owner, as is so commonly done.

Very sincerely yours,
Robert T. Lincoln

Isaac Markens, Esq.
New York, N.Y.

47. "You can fool all the people some of the time and some of the people all of the time, but you can't fool all of the people all of the time." A pronouncement said to have been made by Lincoln at Clinton, Illinois, during the campaign of 1858. There is no contemporary evidence of Lincoln's authorship, and most careful Lincoln students refuse to accept the attribution.

48. William Pitt Kellogg, a lawyer of Canton, Illinois, and a friend and political supporter of Abraham Lincoln. The President appointed him collector of the port of New Orleans, and during Reconstruction he served as governor of Louisiana and United States Senator from that state.

HILDENE, MANCHESTER, VERMONT

November 6, 1917

Dear Mr. Markens:

I am greatly obliged for your kindness in sending me the very pretty copy of the pamphlet about Gettysburg, commemorating "The Lincoln and Burns Event."[49] I am very glad to have it.

Sincerely yours,
Robert T. Lincoln

Isaac Markens, Esq.
New York, New York

49. A program entitled *Presentation and Unveiling of the Memorial Tablets Commemorating The Lincoln and Burns Event (November 19, 1863)*. It contains reminiscences

about Lincoln and John Burns, the old man who shouldered his squirrel rifle and fought in the ranks of the Iron Brigade until he was wounded.

1775 N STREET, WASHINGTON, D.C.

November 26, 1917

Dear Mr. Markens:

I do not think I have acknowledged your letter of November 9th, in regard to the writing by my father of his name in books he owned. I am not greatly surprised to learn from you that there are some which have his name in them, but I am quite sure that I never saw such a thing. I am sorry that I cannot show you the volume of Dr. Smith, "Evidences of Christianity," for I never saw it after I left home for school in 1859, but I remember the book very well.

As to the Scripps' Biography, I cannot certainly speak. I think, however, that there is a reprint of it among my books in Manchester.

In regard to the lecture on "Man," of which you speak in your note of November 15th, I can only say that I do not recall ever having heard of it. I have not ever personally gone through my father's papers, but they were thoroughly examined by Mr. Nicolay, of course, and in later years by my old confidential secretary, Mr. Sweet, who is now dead. I do not think Mr. Nicolay mentions any such lecture, but he does mention others.[50] Mr. Sweet went through the papers carefully, and brought to me from time to time special things which he came across, and I am quite certain that he never showed me any memorandum or manuscript regarding the supposed lecture you mention. That is all I can now say about it.

Very truly yours,

Robert T. Lincoln

50. Lincoln delivered a lecture on Discoveries and Inventions four times in 1858 and 1859. It is probable that this is the lecture to which reference is made here. On March 28, 1859, Lincoln declined an invitation to deliver a lecture at Knox College with the remark, "I read a sort of lecture to three different audiences during the last month and this," which would indicate that Discoveries and Inventions was his sole effort in this field.

1775 N STREET, WASHINGTON, D.C.

December 14, 1917

My dear Mr. Markens:

In regard to getting the photographs you desire, I have sent your request to Mr. Putnam, I do not quite understand your speaking of two drafts of the Gettysburg Address, presented to the Library by Colonel Hay's children. It is my memory that there was only one.[51]

Very truly yours,

Robert T. Lincoln

Isaac Markens, Esq.
New York, New York

51. Here Robert Lincoln was mistaken. The children of John Hay presented two of the five surviving copies of the Gettysburg Address in Lincoln's handwriting to the Library of Congress in 1916.

1775 N STREET, WASHINGTON, D.C.

December 17, 1917

Dear Mr. Markens:

Upon receipt of your letter regarding copies of the Hay manuscripts, I wrote a note to Mr. Putnam, Librarian of Congress, asking about the matter, and saying to him that if something could be done it would give me pleasure to pay the expense of it. I have received a letter from him which encloses a copy of one he wrote you on December 15th, from which you will see that he greatly misunderstood my note.[52] I am consequently asking you by telegraph this morning not to answer his note, but to write to me. It will give me pleasure to have procured for you the photostat prints, which are perfect reproductions, and which I have got for various documents myself. Upon hearing from you in reply to this that you have not ordered the copies, it will give me pleasure to order prints of the manuscripts both for myself and for you, and to send you one set.

Very truly yours,
Robert T. Lincoln

52. Putnam had written to Markens informing him of the charges for photographic and photostatic copies.

1775 N STREET, WASHINGTON, D.C.

December 20, 1917

Dear Mr. Markens:

I have your letter of yesterday, and have at once ordered from the Librarian of Congress two sets of the positive photostats of the Hay drafts of the Gettysburg address, and will send one set to you as soon as received here.

This photostat process is, I am sure, very useful. The only occasion I have taken advantage of it was some years ago having made a copy of a two or three column article on the Bixby letter.

I am very sorry to know that the sickly photograph you speak of is in the War Department, but it is probably buried so deep that it is not a matter of much consequence.

I thank you for the article of Armand de Melun. It is just such an article, I think, that a man adopting such a pen name would write.[53]

Sincerely yours,
Robert T. Lincoln

Isaac Markens, Esq.

53. Neither article nor author has been identified.

1775 N STREET, WASHINGTON, D.C.

December 31, 1917

Dear Mr. Markens:

I return to you the enclosures in your letter of December 27th, in regard to the supposed signature of my father in a law book now in Colorado. I do not, of course, pretend to say that my father never wrote his name in a book belonging to him, but I can only say that I am quite sure I never knew of it myself. I have a few books which he owned and used (not law books), and his name is in none of them. The letter of Dean Fleming[54] says that Lincoln had his own name before that of Mr. Stuart in Volume 3 of the Work.[55] That is curious if true. Major Stuart was the senior of my father in years, and it was he who suggested to my father to study law, and lent to him books for that purpose and took him into a partnership, which lasted some time. The signature of that partnership was Stuart and Lincoln.

The letter you enclosed speaks of Mr. Stuart's letter to Judge Bennett "herewith attached." There is no such letter among your enclosures.

Now as to the tracing pinned to Dean Fleming's letter; it does not at all suggest to me my father's signature.[56] My father's signature was a very clear expression of "A. Lincoln," and so is this tracing, but I do not think the tracing resembles his signature any more than any other neat writing of the same letters would resemble it.

I have just received, and am sending to you separately, the photostat copies of the Hay drafts of the Gettysburg Address. I think I have said to you that I suspect they are two of the writings made in the course of establishing a fixed text for the Gettysburg Address, as told of by Mr. Nicolay.

Very sincerely yours,
Robert T. Lincoln

Isaac Markens, Esq.

54. John D. Fleming, dean of the University of Colorado Law School, 1903–27.
55. Starkie on Evidence, 4th American edition, Philadelphia, 1832.
56. It was, in fact, a crude forgery.

1775 N STREET, WASHINGTON, D.C.

January 4, 1918

Dear Mr. Markens:

I have your note of the 2nd instant, and am glad to know that the photostats reached you safely.

As to the photograph of the old newspaper article relating to the Bixby letter, it is among my papers in Manchester, which are now inaccessible. I remember that it contains stories about the sons, which leads one to think that Mrs. Bixby's maternal loss was not so entire as was indicated in the report upon which my father based his letter, but I cannot now recall the details.[57] I think, however, that it would be rather a pity at this late date to go into that, for it would only distract attention from whatever there is of admiration for the character of the letter itself.

Very truly yours,

Robert T. Lincoln

Isaac Markens, Esq.
New York, New York

57. See p. 36, n. 32.

1775 N STREET, WASHINGTON, D.C.

January 25, 1918

Dear Mr. Markens:

Your note of January 21st with its enclosures has been neglected in the general confusion here. I will attempt to answer your specific inquiries. I never before heard of Forney's statement in regard to my father's having provided for a high and important office to be held by Senator Douglas. As a boy in college, it is not likely that I would have heard of it, even if true, but I doubt its truth. Mr. Douglas' position in the Senate makes the story to me incredible.

Like you, I have often wondered how it happened that my father had so many sittings for photographs. I suppose that the photographers of that time persuaded him to submit to what was then a trial of patience. As to my preference of the Brady photographs, I have always liked the one which was used by Jacques Reich in his well known etching.[58] When it was in process of making he sent me a proof, and I liked it very much, and suggested that he add the profile Remarque. This makes the whole thing more satisfactory to me than any other. As to the exact date of my father's last sitting, I fancy it would be difficult to fix it.[59] I suppose there is little doubt that it occurred after his second Inauguration.

I do not think that there is any probability of publication of any of the papers which you speak of as being in storage. They are, of course, now in my hands. These papers were, as you know, thoroughly gone over by Nicolay and Hay, and I think that in their work they omitted nothing of serious importance.

My brother, William Wallace Lincoln, is buried in the vault of the Lincoln monument at Springfield.[60] His body was taken there from here at the time of my father's funeral.

I have looked over the clippings, and I return them to you with the few comments which follow:

The story of Dr. George Todd is practically correct. I know little of the details of his life, except that he was a surgeon in the Confederate Army, and died in South Carolina.[61] The little inaccuracies of his memory of my father when he was a Member of Congress in 1844 (?) and of his being 6 feet 6 inches tall, are, of course, unimportant.

I know nothing whatever of the story of the soldier's box.

The diamond pin story is ridiculous and wholly untrue. No such thing was ever worn.

The violin story, I think, is equally absurd, and untrue. As to the Emancipation pen, I am unable to say. I knew Rufus S. Andrews very well, and I would think that he believed any story of the sort that he told, but the story itself seems to me to be very improbable in every detail.

The story about the cane is queer. I think I should have remembered any such events as are described in it if they had occurred, and I do not. I do not think there is a word of truth in the story. I do not own any cane ever possessed by my father, and I never took any interest in any such cane. He never used a cane himself at all. At various times in his life there were presented to him canes. I remember such things, but he never cared anything about them, and gave them no attention. I think it is true that after his death my mother gave away to servants some canes which had come to him in Washington, for which none of us had any regard whatever. Such canes may be in existence, but they possess no real interest in connection with my father.

Very sincerely yours,
Robert T. Lincoln

Isaac Markens, Esq.

58. The photograph which Reich used was made by Anthony Berger at Brady's Washington studio on February 9, 1864.

59. The last photographs of Lincoln were taken by Alexander Gardner on April 10, 1865.

60. He died on February 20, 1862.

61. George Rogers Clark Todd was a brother of Mary Todd Lincoln. He served throughout the Civil War as a surgeon in the Confederate army, and after the war practiced in Barnwall, South Carolina. He was not on good terms with the other members of his family.

1775 N STREET, WASHINGTON, D.C.

February 13, 1918

My dear Mr. Markens:

It seems to me the simplest way to answer your letter of February 5th is to return it to you with your interrogatories marked and to make the brief answers to them in this way:

1. The proper answer is that he was a total abstainer, but on two or three occasions in my life, not more, I have seen him take a sip of a glass of ale and also of a glass of champagne. On each occasion he was urged to do this as a tonic. I do not think it ever occurred to him of his own motion to drink anything except water or tea or coffee or milk. As you know, he always was a strong temperance advocate.

2. The Bloomington shipment you refer to is no doubt the boxes of papers which Judge Davis took charge of, as administrator of my father's estate, and caused to be removed to Bloomington, his home, where he had a safe storage place for them. They remained unopened until given over to Nicolay and Hay for their work. They are now in my possession.

3. I heard nothing of this while in London, but I have in some way understood that in one of the college libraries, whether in Oxford or in Cambridge I do not know, is hanging framed a lithographed copy of the Bixby letter. As to the Gettysburg address and opinions of English publications thereon, I have not now any present memory.

4. His methods of office working were simply those of a very busy man who worked at all hours. He never dictated correspondence; he sometimes wrote a document and had his draft copied by either Nicolay or Hay; sometimes he himself copied his corrected draft and retained the draft in his papers; there were no letter press books at all; he never owned such a thing. When he preserved letters to himself, it was ordinarily done by replacing them in their envelopes with the writer's name inscribed; it was not his general habit to keep copies of letters written by himself.

5. I know nothing whatever about this.[62]

6. This letter is in my possession.[63]

7. I never heard of any picture of my grandfather, Thomas Lincoln.

I trust that you are very well and are enjoying some comfort as we are from the change in the dreadful weather of this winter.

Very truly yours,
Robert T. Lincoln

Isaac Markens, Esq.
545 West 164th St.
New York City

---

62. Markens' question: "Can you tell anything more definite than that of Nicolay, on the question of President Lincoln's preference of Andrew Johnson for the Vice Presidency in 1864, or any other facts relating to the matter?"

63. Markens had asked: "Can you tell me the whereabouts of the letter of Queen Victoria to your mother?"

1775 N STREET, WASHINGTON, D.C.

March 5, 1918

Dear Mr. Markens:

I have your letter of February 27th; I do not think I can help you much in regard to your inquiries about President Lincoln's way of holding his hands. I do not think he had any special way of holding his hands. Of course I have seen him under all circumstances, but I never saw him standing as though he was holding down a cramp with his hands. I saw him on some of the speech making occasions you mention and at every one of them I think he had in one hand his manuscript, which settled the use of one hand at least. Curiously I never saw him receiving a delegation at the White House.

Like you, I do not believe that Mr. Welles ever resigned or proposed to do so, and I do not believe that he ever received a slight from my father. His diary was a very full and particular account of his experiences in Washington and it is not my recollection that there is anything in it to indicate such a situation. I myself read the diary in manuscript from beginning to end. In the publication of it by his son there were some things omitted, but nothing of importance. I have the diary in my house in the country so that I cannot conveniently make any reference to it here, but I should be surprised to find any indication in it to justify the information of which you write.

I have never seen Rothschild's last book and have never felt interested in it enough to do so. I have myself seen very few comments on it and I have had the feeling that it had attracted very little attention.

I thank you for your good wishes and am glad to tell you that we are pretty well without any serious results from the bad winter which happily seems to have come to an end.

Very sincerely yours,
Robert T. Lincoln

Isaac Markens, Esq.
New York City

1775 N STREET, WASHINGTON, D.C.

April 6, 1918

Dear Mr. Markens:

I am a little shocked to find how long it is that I have let remain unanswered your letter of March 11th, but I have been extremely busy and have neglected much of my correspondence.

You ask in it about so many things that it is not easy to answer, but I can deal with some of them. Our family bible is in my closed-up house in Manchester. It contains an entry, as I remember by my father, of my mother's birthday, of which I now remember only the year, 1818.[64] I am told by my aunt, the only surviving child of my grandfather Todd, that my mother's birthday was December 13, 1818, and I may mention that my aunt is a great stickler on correct statistics. If you correctly quote the expression in the letter written by my mother, I can only account for the discrepancy by the unhappy mental condition in which she lived during the years following my father's death.

I do not remember at all any person named "Gumpert," to whom my brother Tad's letter was addressed. Thomas Cross, whom you speak of, was a colored servant, who did not permit himself to be forgotten by me for many years. This letter was written by a boy eleven years old and is of course very crude. I fancy the carriage bill refers to a cart he used with a goat. There may have been some person named Gumpert in the Company which furnished the House sentinels, but I do not know.[65] I can tell you nothing about Mr. Ervin Chapman's statement about a visit of President Lincoln to Henry Ward Beecher in Brooklyn. I have no doubt that Nicolay's statement to you is entirely correct. I have not read Mr. Chapman's recent book,[66] but there came to me a little while ago a clipping from the Los Angeles Times containing an article by him entitled "Misconceptions of Abraham Lincoln," which began with a statement as to myself (calling me the second son of my father!) which I have cut from it and beg you will return to me in the enclosed envelope as I may wish to use it again.

Mr. Chapman happened to catch me in Chicago a few years ago and I had a pleasant chat with him. I do not remember it particularly, but it is entirely possible that in answer to a question I explained to him my understanding of the position of my father's grandfather in Kentucky, which was this: He had settled in Rockingham County, Virginia, where he owned land which he cultivated as a farmer. In the early migration to Kentucky, he sold his farm and with the money in his pocket went to Kentucky; it certainly was no great sum. He settled in Kentucky as a pioneer and bought from the Governor of Virginia a very considerable amount of land which I suppose he paid for. I happen to have one of the land patents to him. While cultivating a part of his land on which it happens as I am told there is now located the Union Railway Station of Louisville, Kentucky, and being in company with one of his sons, who was a youth, and also by his very small son, who became my father's father, he was attacked by one or more Indians and was shot dead. The older son ran to the neighboring cabin, seized his rifle and shot an Indian dead who was carrying off the very young son. This enabled the older son to rush out and save his young brother. As I understand it, besides the inconsiderable personal belongings of a farmer, the entire estate of the slain man consisted of his patented land in Kentucky, and he having made no will, this land went under the then existing law of *primo geniture* to his oldest son, and the young son was left penniless.

Mr. Chapman's account of this story is absurd in representing me as saying that the emigrant was one of the richest men in Virginia and that he was the owner of more than 5000 acres of land. Such statements are absurd and were never made or thought by me, and I suppose they may at some time be quoted as one indication of my folly.[67] I do not know whether what I have spoken of is in his book or not, but I hope not.

Upon your question what it was President Cleveland said in admiration of President Lincoln told in a letter to me by Mr. Gilder, I cannot imagine what it is you refer to. I probably have at Manchester all of Mr. Gilder's letters to me, and I will endeavor to look this up when I return there next month.

Nor do I know what it is that Mr. Gilder describes as "stupendous things" related to him when he paid me a visit. I probably told him of some conversations with my father, particularly one relating to the Battle of Gettysburg, and if so, they related to things which are denied by others, and of which there is no existing evidence except my memory. I shall most certainly not by any further publication of my own venture to raise a discussion which could have no good result and would be a great bore to me.

This is a very scrappy letter, but it could not well avoid being so.

Trusting you are quite well, I am,

Very sincerely yours,

Robert T. Lincoln

Isaac Markens, Esq.

64. This Bible is now in the Rare Book Division of the Library of Congress. Among other entries in Lincoln's hand is one indicating that he and Mary Todd were married on November 4, 1842. Above Lincoln's name is a pencilled entry: "b. Feb. 12, 1809"; and above her name: "b. Dec. 12, 1818." The Chicago Historical Society has sections of a Lincoln family Bible with entries in Abraham Lincoln's handwriting. There the date of Mary Todd's birth is given as December 13, 1818. This date has been accepted by all biographers.

65. Gustav Edward Gumpert was a friend of Tad Lincoln's who lived in Philadelphia. The communication to which allusion is made is identified by Ruth Painter Randall: "On October 6, 1864, on the official stationery of the Executive Mansion was written in a far from well-trained handwriting the following telegram: 'Dear Gumpert: I send Thomas Cross to see you about the Carriage Bill. It was Sent, to me Aand I ant got any money to pay the man with And Oblidge Thomas Lincoln Yur Friend Tad[.]'" *Lincoln's Sons* (Boston, 1955), p. 197.

66. The Rev. Dr. Ervin Chapman (1838–1921) held pastorates in the United Brethren of Christ, Presbyterian, and Congregational churches. His two-volume *Latest Light on Abraham Lincoln* (New York, Chicago, Toronto) was published in 1917. In Vol. II, pp. 535–38, he related a story which he attributed to Samuel Scoville, Jr., grandson of Henry Ward Beecher. According to Scoville, Mrs. Beecher told him that shortly after the Battle of Bull Run a stranger in a military cloak visited the Beecher home in Brooklyn. He did not reveal his identity to Mrs. Beecher, but spent several hours with her husband. Twenty years later, Scoville said, Beecher revealed that his visitor had been Abraham Lincoln, come "to gain the sympathy and help of one whom he knew as a man of God." The story has not been credited by critical biographers.

67. The estate of Abraham Lincoln, grandfather of the President, was appraised at sixty-eight pounds, sixteen shillings, and sixpence, including two horses, six head of cattle, pewter plates, and three feather-beds. The grandfather's land-holdings, inherited by his eldest son Mordecai, comprised 5,544 acres. Louis A. Warren, *Lincoln's Parentage and Childhood* (New York, 1926), p. 11.

1775 N STREET, WASHINGTON, D.C.

April 8, 1918

My dear Mr. Markens:

Here is something which I forgot to send you in my last letter. The enclosed clipping from the New York Sun of January 6th last attracted my attention on account of the pretended literal documentary accuracy, and in order to see what possible basis there could be for the absurd story as to a document written by President Lincoln, I wrote at once to the newspaper, the Reading Eagle, in which I made the necessary particular inquiries about it. The typewritten note enclosed was the reply I received mentioning the cutting which is also enclosed. It is seen from this that the whole thing is a fake for which there is no foundation except the senile maunderings of an old soldier. It may be possible that my father somewhere saw him and was attracted by his unusual height. The rest of the story is unbelievable, but some idiots might think it to be a piece of documentary history.[68] I have thought it might interest you to have it.

Very sincerely yours,
Robert T. Lincoln

Isaac Markens, Esq.

68. The *New York Sun* of January 6, 1918 had reprinted a story from the *Reading Eagle* of December 27, 1917 in which a former soldier, Mahlon Shaaber of the 93rd Pennsylvania Infantry, told how Lincoln had once called him out of the ranks and recorded his unusual height (six feet, six and one-half inches) in a pocket notebook. In reply to Robert Lincoln's request for documentary evidence the city editor of the *Reading Eagle* had to admit that none existed.

3014 N STREET, WASHINGTON, D.C.

June 18, 1918

Dear Mr. Markens:

Your note of June 14th was forwarded to me from Manchester, where we have not yet arrived. I am expecting to leave within a day or two to go there for the summer.

I am afraid that I can tell you nothing about my father's handwriting that you probably do not know. In the first volume of Nicolay & Hay are two lithographs, the first of which, if genuine, indicates his handwriting at the age of about sixteen. The next is a lithograph of a report on a road survey. It is unmistakably genuine and shows clearly the handwriting he had acquired at the age of twenty-five and the handwriting which he used throughout his after life. As you say, there are no noteworthy added peculiarities or changes. As to the pens he used, I cannot actually remember, but in early life he must have used quills, as everybody did in our part of the country. In later life he used steel pens entirely, and the character of the pen he used is sufficiently shown in the writing itself. He was a very deliberate writer, anything but rapid. I cannot remember any peculiarity about his posture; he wrote sitting at a table and, as I remember, in an ordinary posture. As to dictation, I never saw him dictate to anyone, and it certainly was not his practice to do so. He seemed to think nothing of the labor of writing personally and was accustomed to make many scraps of notes or memoranda. In writing a careful letter, he first wrote it himself, then corrected it, and then rewrote the corrected version himself. You must remember that there were in those days practically no private stenographers. I do not now recall having seen any letter written either by Nicolay or by Hay which was personally signed by him.

There is an instance of my father's direct dictation at page 291, Volume III, Nicolay and Hay, where Nicolay wrote out from dictation a part of my father's short speech made at the train as he was leaving Springfield.[69]

I am afraid that this is all I can tell you on the subject.

Very sincerely yours,

Robert T. Lincoln

Isaac Markens, Esq.

69. After the train started Lincoln began to write out what he had said but soon gave up because of the jouncing of the car. Nicolay took over and completed the record.

HILDENE, MANCHESTER, VERMONT

July 9, 1918

Dear Mr. Markens:

I find that, in the confusion of moving from Washington here, among the things I did not bring was a letter from you in regard to the birthday of my mother. The matter, however, came to my mind this morning, and I examined the family Bible in which the original entries were made by my father, beginning with his marriage. I find that many years ago I made a pencilled note in that entry giving the date of my mother's birth as December 12, 1818. I do not recall the basis on which I then made it, but it was undoubtedly carefully done, and I have no doubt of its correctness.[70] I have already given you my explanation of the curious statement in her letter, which you quoted to me.

Very sincerely yours,
Robert T. Lincoln

Isaac Markens, Esq.

70. See p. 58 and n. 64.

HILDENE, MANCHESTER, VERMONT

July 13, 1918

Dear Mr. Markens:

Your letter of the 10th only reaches me this morning and I will try at once to dispose of the several matters you write about. I shall be very glad to see Professor Robinson's forthcoming book.[71]

I have no idea of the source of the words in my father's letter to Mrs. Browning.[72]

As to my father's "anxiety and woe-begone appearance during the war" being much exaggerated, I can only say that I do not think I saw any change in him. There were occasions that I remember when he was much distressed and plainly exhibited his feelings. One of those occasions was when he learned of General Fitz-John Porter's conduct at the second battle of Bull Run;[73] the other was when he learned of Lee's successful recrossing of the river after the battle of Gettysburg. Unless for some special reason, he did not during the war seem to me unduly anxious or distressed.

In regard to the cane business, I suppose I have written to you that he never used a cane. That is true so far as I know. Various canes were presented to him, but I never saw one in his hand. Herndon's circumstantial statement on any subject does not create the slightest impression of truth in my mind. It is not at all within my recollection that he was present at the first Inauguration, and I am sure that I never saw him in Washington. As to the President's thought about his place in history, I know nothing on which to base a suggestion which is not open to everyone.

In regard to the photograph taken on the deck of Schley's flag-ship "Thetis," I do not think that I ever saw it. I certainly have nothing of the sort among my belongings. In fact, I have not the slightest memory of one being taken. I do remember waving a farewell to Captain Schley as his ship was going down stream.[74]

I do not quite understand your implied criticism of Dr. Hibben's saying in his Lincoln Centennial Association address in 1917 that Lincoln's Gettysburg address and his second Inaugural were quoted in Scotland the "first month of the war" by Dr. McGregor.[75] What is wrong about that?

I am glad to tell you that I am feeling far better this year than a year ago, but we do not seem to be having the delightful weather of which you speak. We are having too much rain for our pleasure.

Trusting that you are yourself very well, I am

Very sincerely yours,

Robert T. Lincoln

Isaac Markens, Esq.

71. *Abraham Lincoln as a Man of Letters*, by Luther E. Robinson (Chicago, 1918).
72. A jocular, tasteless, and self-deprecating letter about his courtship of Mary

Owens which Lincoln wrote to Mrs. Orville H. Browning on April 1, 1838. *The Collected Works of Abraham Lincoln*, I, 117–18.

73. Porter, commanding the V Corps of Pope's Army of Virginia, was accused of disobedience and misconduct in the face of the enemy at the Second Battle of Bull Run. He was found guilty and cashiered on January 21, 1863. In 1879, when a board of general officers reviewed his case, he was exonerated.

74. Captain, later Rear Admiral, Winfield Scott Schley (1839–1911) commanded the relief expedition that rescued Army Lieutenant A. W. Greely and six of his men who survived a disastrous exploration of the Arctic in 1884.

75. Dr. John Grier Hibben, president of Princeton University, had said: "In Scotland during the first month of the war [World War I] Dr. McGregor in St. Andrews Church in Edinburgh in three successive sermons quoted from Lincoln's Gettysburg address and his second Inaugural, and entreated his hearers 'to practice in this day the patience, the charity, the gentle humanity of the great American who led his country through troublous times to victory.' "

HILDENE, MANCHESTER, VERMONT

August 2, 1918

Dear Mr. Markens:

I thank you very much for your kind note which came yesterday.[76] I am glad to tell you that it found me in very good trim and able to enjoy a game of golf in beautiful weather.

With all good wishes, believe me

Very sincerely yours,

Robert T. Lincoln

Isaac Markens, Esq.

76. Undoubtedly a note of congratulations on the recipient's seventy-fifth birthday, August 1.

HILDENE, MANCHESTER, VERMONT

Nov. 5th, 1918

Dear Mr. Markens:

Your letter came several days after my household goods freight car had started on its way to Washington, having in it the Index Book of all my Files here; I have made a little search but have failed to light on the box having the Benson package. I do not think however that I could answer your inquiry from anything in it; I recall clearly that Benson seemed to be a wanderer and that my last news of him indicated that he had been a member of the Front-Hall servants party at the White House when I had a talk with Colonel Hay about the lithograph, when he suggested to me the easy possibility of its having been made from a forgery. I had already become satisfied that Benson was "no good," and gave no more thought to him. It is in my memory that I saw his name about that time in a Government publication, then called the Blue Book I think. He might be traced through that, perhaps, if it were worth while, which I doubt.[77]

My Lincoln papers are in Washington; when I get there I will with pleasure try to find something for you.

The Bixby-Kaiser Letters comparison is quite interesting; it shows very different mental attitudes.

I shall in a few days leave here for Washington, via Chicago, and will write you from there. I am glad to infer that you have escaped the influenza, as we have happily done.

Very truly yours,

Robert T. Lincoln

77. See pp. 34–36 and n. 32.

3014 N STREET, WASHINGTON, D.C.

February 1st, 1919

Dear Mr. Markens:

I came here about the middle of November and have been and still am in the greatest confusion that I have ever known; we are repairing a very old house while camping in it and it is a far more tedious job than I feared. Next Monday the old entrance steps are to be torn away and I suppose that for a week or so we shall enter our front door by a kitchen step-ladder. I lost my secretary and could not replace him and have been at my wit's end trying to get through an unusual lot of work which I could not neglect. The result is that my table is piled up with all sorts of letters and I am almost disheartened. I can only ask your pardon for letting several of your notes lie in the heap and will now try to write you.

I return your note of November 30th, having attached the Drinkwater article which I have read with a melancholy interest; I must say frankly that I do not like such efforts as his.[78] There was a man named Chapin, I think, whose publicity was extremely distasteful to me. I believe he is now dead but unhappily he is survived by a movie film, of which I have only seen shocking posters.[79] There is now on my table photographs of a Chicago man who asks my advice as to the best way of getting himself on the stage as an impersonator of Lincoln; he will not get it. Then an old broken down painter is belaboring me to give him sittings of advice to enable him to create the greatest in the World portrait of Lincoln. And so it goes.

I cannot certainly make out the name of the man of whom you write as having "seen my father off" at Springfield but I do not think it is any name known to me.

I have had my file of Benson papers sent me from Vermont and enclose to you an abstract of my relations with him, which ended some sixteen years ago; I have no idea of his address. I think that if he were still alive he would be trying to pull my leg in some way.

Recalling his pretended Bixby letter, of which he issued a lithograph, I do not know whether I have ever told you that Mr. Judd Stewart (q. v. Who's Who in America,) has two Bixby letter lithographs, in one of which "assuage" is spelled "assauge." One of them must be a forgery, probably the other is simply an amended forgery. I have given up all hope of discovering the original letter.

I am not forgetting the scrap of paper you wish but simply cannot in the present confusion here look it up just now; I will do so very soon.

Very sincerely yours,
Robert T. Lincoln

78. The reference is to a long review of John Drinkwater's play, "Abraham Lincoln," first produced at Birmingham, England, in 1918. (The American premier did not take place until November 23, 1919, nearly ten months after the date of this letter.) The review, signed by H. W. Massingham and credited to *The London Nation*, was reprinted in an American paper which cannot now be identified or dated. One can guess that Robert Lincoln disapproved of any distortion of the facts of his father's life in the name of dramatic license, and can be sure that he was angered by Massingham's question and answer, "Did he [Lincoln] ever love a woman? It is doubtful."

79. Benjamin C. Chapin (1875–1918) was an actor-writer who made a career of impersonating Abraham Lincoln. Chapin appeared as Lincoln in vaudeville, the theater, and films. The films included "Son of Democracy" and the "Benjamin Chapin Cycle of Lincoln Photoplays." The posters that offended Robert Lincoln were probably those produced in 1919 to promote "Son of Democracy." Eleven of these posters in the Chicago Historical Society include "Abe Defends the Pickaniny," "Abe earns his first Dime," and "His Mother. He learned to write that famous name."

HILDENE, MANCHESTER, VERMONT

August 19, 1919

Dear Mr. Markens:

I ought long ago to have thanked you for your kind remembrance of my most _____ birthday.[80] It found me in fairly good trim.

I trust that you are quite well.

Very truly yours,
Robert T. Lincoln

80. In this holograph note the word before "birthday" is indecipherable.

3014 N STREET, WASHINGTON, D.C.

May 29, 1920

Dear Mr. Markens:

In answer to your inquiry, the portrait of my father made by Matthew Wilson in 1865, for Secretary Welles, was well known to me. Upon the death of Mr. Welles it passed to his son, Edgar T. Welles, who died a few years ago in New York City. The picture then being owned by his daughter, Miss Alice Welles, was later sold by her, but I have no memorandum here of the name of the purchaser.[81] I knew it at the time. The address of Miss Welles is 54 East 57th Street, New York City.

Very truly yours,

Robert T. Lincoln

81. L. C. Prang & Company of Boston commissioned London-born Matthew Wilson in 1865 to paint a portrait of Lincoln for reproduction as a lithograph. Later, Wilson told a friend that Lincoln gave him one sitting before the assassination. Wilson completed the portrait from photographs, and the lithograph made from it was circulated widely. Rufus Rockwell Wilson, *Lincoln in Portraiture* (New York, 1935), p. 283.

Apparently Gideon Welles, Secretary of the Navy, acquired the original Wilson portrait, and a copy made by the artist went to Lincoln's old friend, Joshua Speed. "50 Contemporary Lincoln Portrait Painters," *Lincoln Lore*, June 5, 1944.

HILDENE, MANCHESTER, VERMONT

August 2, 1920

Dear Mr. Markens:

I thank you very much for your good wishes on my numerous [sic] anniversary. I find myself started on a new year in fairly good trim and shall try to keep in good order.

I can not understand why your letter to Miss Alice Welles should have been returned to you as "not found," for I could hardly have made an error in her address. She lives with her aunt, the wife of Mr. W. R. Mowe, at 54 East 67th Street, New York. I think you wished to write her about a portrait of my father, which came to her from her father, it having been painted for her grandfather Secretary Welles. Perhaps when I wrote you I was unable to give you the information you desire. I can now tell you that the painting was made by Matthew Wilson, an artist of English birth, who was born in 1814 and died in Brooklyn in 1892. He spent a good deal of his time in Philadelphia and was, I understand, a well known artist. In 1915 Miss Welles received an offer for the painting from a Mr. Hart, who, as I understand, was a collector, and Miss Welles held him out for a pretty stiff price. I do not know whether Mr. Hart still owns the picture or has disposed of it in someway.

I trust that you are very well, and with all good wishes,

Believe me,

Very sincerely yours,

Robert T. Lincoln

Isaac Markens.

RL/DK

P.S. In Vol. X of Who's Who in America (1918–1919) is a notice of Charles Henry Hart, who bought the Wilson portrait.[82]

82. Charles Henry Hart (1847–1918), originally a lawyer, became an expert in art and historical portraiture. He was director of the Pennsylvania Academy of Fine Arts, 1882–1902. Among his many writings were three concerning Lincoln: *Bibliographia Lincolniana* (1870), *A Biographical Sketch of His Excellency Abraham Lincoln* (1870), and *Catalogue of a Collection of Engraved and other Portraits of Lincoln* (1899).

HILDENE, MANCHESTER, VERMONT

August 12, 1920

Dear Mr. Markens:

Miss Alice Welles has sent to me your recent letter to her, making inquiry about the Wilson picture, and which has evidently bothered her a good deal. Miss Welles is a young woman, I am not even sure that she ever saw her grandfather Secretary Welles. She knows nothing whatever of the circumstances attending the painting of my father's portrait for Secretary Welles in 1865. It was simply a possession that came from her grandfather to her own father, and the latter had no special information about it. He died several years ago. Miss Welles says to me that it would not please her to indicate the price that she got for the picture. You are in error in supposing that it was a long drawn out affair. Mr. Hart made her an offer for it, she thought she should have a larger price and she made in answer to him an offer to sell the picture at a certain price, which Mr. Hart promptly accepted. I think that she is entirely right in not wishing to give the price she got, without the consent of Mr. Hart, and there is no reason why she should ask that consent.

I am feeling that I committed an indiscretion in not saying this to you before, and I am therefore, venturing to say to you now that I am writing to Miss Welles saying to her that I have written to you and that she need not acknowledge your letter. This will explain your not hearing from her.

Your very sincerely,
Robert T. Lincoln

RL/DK

HILDENE, MANCHESTER, VERMONT

August 26, 1920

Dear Mr. Markens:

I have been delayed in acknowledging your letter of August 5th. It is quite impossible for Miss Welles to give you the information about the Wilson portrait which you wish. She was not born until long after it was painted. I do not think it a matter of much consequence to have a controversy with Mr. Thorpe, but if you wish to know something more about the Wilson picture I can tell you, that Mr. Wilson was born in England in 1814 and died in Brooklyn in 1892. A son of his, Mr. Francis A. Wilson, was for a long time a cashier of the Farmers Loan and Trust Company of New York City, but is now retired and lives at 45 Sidney Place, Brooklyn, New York. He writes me saying, "My understanding is that father was engaged by Secretary Welles to paint for him a portrait of your [my] father, now in possession of Miss Welles, and which I believe was executed two weeks before President Lincoln's death."

As you intimate, I did not think much of Mr. Thorpe's painting of my father which he showed me, perhaps a year ago. The head was made from a Brady photograph and was, of course, recognizable, but as a work of art the canvas was very bad. As I recall the costume of black looked as though it had been made by a house painter's brush over a stencil, and that there was no attempt at shading.

I have no special opinion of the newspaper picture of myself to which you refer. It was not taken at my house but on the street here by a persistent reporter whom I had attempted to dodge but he seems to have caught me at a time I did not know he was about. I have no copies of it, except some sent me by friends from various parts of the country. I should not care to autograph one of them, nor can I send you any photograph of myself for I have none at all. I have not sat for a photograph for more than twenty years I think, and I have no intention of doing so again.

The autograph of my father which you have seen in the Chicago Historical Society, is one that I know nothing about. The Charles Forbes who makes an affidavit as to its genuineness was my father's carriage footman, and I remember him as a very good fellow in his place but I have not heard of him in many years and I suppose he is no longer living.

Believe me,

Sincerely yours,
Robert T. Lincoln

Isaac Markens, Esq.
1416 Olive Avenue
Chicago, Ill.
RL/DK

HILDENE, MANCHESTER, VERMONT

September 7th, 1920

Dear Mr. Markens:

I have your letter regarding an autograph of my father on a card hanging in the Evanston Public Library, as to which you express doubt on account of its date. Assuming the genuineness of the card, the explanation of the date seems to me to be simple. It is quite impossible that my father wrote such a note to the Secretary of the Navy on January 3, 1861, but we all know that one has to be careful in the early days of January to avoid writing the number of the just passed year. This is, I am sure, merely an instance of such a slip.

Very sincerely yours,
Robert T. Lincoln

Isaac Markens, Esq.

HILDENE, MANCHESTER, VERMONT

November 3, 1920

Dear Mr. Markens:

I never before heard of the alleged offer by Mr. Corning, to my father, after he had made his speech at the Cooper Institute, and I do not for a moment believe there is any foundation for the statement.[83]

Major James B. Merwin, whom you mentioned, died about three years ago, at the age of eighty-five. My father made him a Hospital Chaplain in 1862, and he dropped out in 1865. He wrote a book, which I cannot now lay my hand on, which led me to think that he was a very good, well meaning man, but that he could not be at all depended upon for his statements. They were not harmful, but they indicated a vivid imagination. For instance, he tells of a considerably extended temperance campaign conducted by my father in Illinois, in which he accompanied him. That, in my opinion, is mere fiction. At the time he speaks of, my father was devoting all the time he could spare from his work, in his anti-Nebraska campaign, in Illinois.

Merwin pretends to give quotations from him as though he were a stenographer, which he certainly was not. I think he was a man who intruded himself upon prominent people, and they did a great many things for him to get rid of him. I think he probably got in his dotage, and that the statement you refer to, is one of the results of that.[84]

Very truly yours,
Robert T. Lincoln

RTL:M

83. Erastus Corning, president of the New York Central Railroad, 1853–1864, is said to have offered Lincoln the position of the road's general counsel after he made his Cooper Union address. Most biographers have been as skeptical as Robert Lincoln.

84. Merwin's account of Lincoln's temperance activities was printed in many places, and disbelieved by all except zealots in the cause of prohibition. Robert Lincoln had a sure instinct for spotting frauds.

3014 N STREET, WASHINGTON, D.C.

December 14, 1920

Dear Mr. Markens:

In reply to your note I can only say that I do not recall any recorded expression of President Arthur in regard to my father and I doubt if there is any available. President Arthur was a charming man for whom I had a great affection and grieved greatly at his untimely death. I do not believe that you can make any addition to your article on his account.

Sincerely yours,

Robert T. Lincoln

Isaac Markens, Esq.
New York, N.Y.

3014 N STREET, WASHINGTON, D.C.

January 19, 1921

My dear Mr. Markens:

Your letter of the 15th instant comes to me this morning. I am sorry that it is quite impossible for me to give of my own knowledge any information respecting my father's acquaintance with, or opinion of, any of the presidents you name in your letter beyond what you evidently know yourself from your studies, and I know of no source of information beyond what can be found in Nicolay and Hay's Life and the two supplemental volumes. Nor can I answer your question as to whether he met Andrew Johnson after the latter's inauguration as Vice President. I happened to be in the Senate chamber when Mr. Johnson made his rather famous inaugural address.[85] I myself returned immediately to City Point and have no knowledge of any meeting after that. As to their personal relations I have no knowledge except what is to be gained from the well known history of the Baltimore Convention in 1864. I was, of course, a very young man at the time, and I do not recollect my father ever speaking to me about Mr. Johnson.

Very truly yours,
Robert T. Lincoln

Isaac Markens, Esq.
New York, N.Y.

85. Andrew Johnson, recovering from an illness, had braced himself for the inaugural ceremonies with an over-generous dosage of liquor. He was obviously drunk when he made his inaugural address. Johnson was not an habitual drunkard, or even an habitual drinker.

3014 N STREET, WASHINGTON, D.C.

February 16, 1921

Dear Mr. Markens:

I have no copy of the picture you refer to except a small photograph which was sent me by the Secretary of the Chicago Historical Society, and my only reason for getting it was that it explains the pose of a large portrait of my father. I regard the photograph as of so little importance that in my house it is slipped behind the frame of the large portrait. There was such a meeting as it indicates,[86] but the arrangement of the figures came from the imagination of Mr. Healy, the Artist.

Very truly yours,
Robert T. Lincoln

Isaac Markens, Esq.

86. The "River Queen" conference between Lincoln, Grant, Sherman, and Admiral Porter was held on the steamer of that name at City Point, Virginia, on March

27, 1865. G. P. A. Healy made a famous painting of the scene, and several separate paintings of Lincoln as he was pictured in the group.

3014 N STREET, WASHINGTON, D.C.

March 29, 1921

Dear Mr. Markens:

I have been very much occupied and have in consequence allowed your note in regard to the Leet portrait of my father with spectacles in his lap to be somewhat neglected. I made one call there some time ago when Mr. Leet was not in and let the matter drop until recently. I have now procured from them and have the pleasure of enclosing you a print of the photograph you desire. It is a very good picture, but I do not know who made it.[87]

In regard to Congressman Yates' reference to William Pitt Kellogg, I have no personal knowledge and have nothing at hand to inform myself.[88]

Trusting that you are very well, I am,

Sincerely yours,

Robert T. Lincoln

Isaac Markens, Esq.

87. The photograph is attributed to Alexander Gardner, and was probably made on August 9, 1863. Leet Brothers, photographic copyists in Washington, claimed to have an old glass negative from which they made numerous sepia-tone prints.

88. Congressman Richard Yates of Illinois related a story about his father Richard Yates, Governor of Illinois, 1861–65, and U.S. Senator, 1865–71, in a Lincoln's birthday speech in the House of Representatives, February 12, 1921. Yates said: "On the morning of the day of the assassination, a visit to the White House was paid by my father, then a senator, and another Illinoisan, who had been a presidential elector, and later a Federal judge, and later a colonel of the Seventh Illinois Cavalry. My father said, 'Mr. President, here is the man you want.' The President said, 'That's so, he'll do,' and added, 'I am going to send you to New Orleans to be collector of the port—you will have 2,000 employees under you, all northerners, because substantially all southerners are disfranchised; but I want you to make love to those people down there.' . . . . It is of interest to record that at this interview the President, for some reason, said: 'I want this commission issued now,' and did not rest until the commission was de-

livered—sent over by the Secretary of the Treasury—and the two Illinoisans walked out with the last commission ever signed by Lincoln." . . . Yates's friend was William Pitt Kellogg. See also p. 46 and notes 47 and 48.

HILDENE, MANCHESTER, VERMONT

August 5, 1921

Dear Mr. Markens:

I thank you very much for your kind remembrance to me on my recent birthday. I am sorry to tell you that this one finds me somewhat out of trim, but I am hoping to feel better very soon. I trust you may have the same good fortune.

Believe me,

Very sincerely yours,
Robert T. Lincoln

Isaac Markens, Esq.
562 West 161 Street
New York, New York

HILDENE, MANCHESTER, VERMONT

October 27, 1921

Dear Mr. Markens:

I have delayed answering your note of October 20th about the Fuchs portrait because the photograph of it arrived only yesterday, and only one photograph came which, of course, I want to keep. I am sorry to say I am writing to Mr. Fuchs that I do not think the photograph is a good one of the portrait, which we think as good as is possible. I should, of course, be pleased to send you a photograph of the picture, but the situation is an odd one. It was painted upon the instigation of some friends and I only know the name of one of them. It is planned as I understand it to be placed in the Golf Club here, but I have no information whatever as to when it is to be done, or how it is to be arranged for. This may seem to you a curious situation, but it is the situation, and I am not quite in a position to clear it up.

Mr. Fuchs did not come here to paint my portrait. It was to execute a commission for the portrait of Captain Hunt, upon the order of an Engineering Society of New York, and the making of my portrait was an incident which occurred to me as a great surprise, and I do not yet understand all the circumstances.[89]

I have several papers in regard to the Proctor incident, as to which I shall write you when I am a little better prepared to do so.

Very sincerely yours,
Robert T. Lincoln

89. The oil portrait of Robert Todd Lincoln by Emil Fuchs, Vienna-born painter, hung for a time in the Mark Skinner Library in Manchester, but is now in storage.

HILDENE, MANCHESTER, VERMONT

November 15, 1922

Dear Mr. Markens:

Your note of November 13th just comes to me as I am almost at the end of my packing to leave here for the winter so that I must write you very hastily.

I do not remember any Mr. West, but I have in my hand an old volume called "Early Settlers of Sangamon County" by J. C. Power. It is a crude work but of some value. I find in it an account of Benjamin West born in 1812 in Boston, studied at the law school of Harvard in 1836 and came to Sangamon County at that time, settling at Rochester. He was a lawyer and was one of the representatives of Sangamon County in the State Legislature of 1846 and 47. He died on June 23, 1847. He had one son born in 1845 who was educated in the Lutheran College in Spring-field but went to New Hampshire and from there went to the Philippine Islands where in 1863 he was drowned in a wreck.

That is all I can tell you of Benjamin West and I think it would take a great deal of difficult inquiry to learn any more about him.

Very sincerely yours,
Robert T. Lincoln

Isaac Markens, Esq.
555 West 160th St.
New York City, N.Y.
RTL:G

3014 N STREET, WASHINGTON, D.C.

February 28, 1924

Isaac Markens, Esquire
    545 West 164th Street
    New York City
Dear Mr. Markens:

Receipt is acknowledged of your letter of the 26th instant in which you refer to a controversy now being carried on between certain parties as to the present whereabouts of the last suit of clothes worn by President Lincoln and ask me for information on the subject. As I do not care to attempt to decide this controversy, and have no authentic data bearing upon it, I beg that you will excuse me from making any comment whatsoever about the matter.

With best wishes, believe me,

Very truly yours,
Robert T. Lincoln

HILDENE, MANCHESTER, VERMONT

June 6, 1924

Isaac Markens, Esquire
    545 West 164th Street
    New York City
Dear Mr. Markens:

I am in receipt of your letter of the 3rd instant informing me of the loss of the little picture of my son which I gave you some years ago. I am very sorry to say that I have not in my possession at this time a duplicate of this photograph which I could send you, but I trust that you will find the picture which has been lost in due course.

Very truly yours,
Robert T. Lincoln

HILDENE, MANCHESTER, VERMONT

July 29th, 1924

Isaac Markens, Esquire
    545 West 164th Street
    New York City
My dear Mr. Markens:

I am in receipt of your letter of recent date requesting certain information in regard to the papers which I have deposited with the Library of Congress under a Special Trust agreement providing that they shall not be made public until after my death.

While I cannot accurately estimate the number of these papers, in a general way they embrace simply some of the personal correspondence and papers of my father. There are no portraits in the collection, nor are there any printed documents.[90]

Believe me,

Very truly yours,
Robert T. Lincoln

90. Robert Lincoln deposited eight trunks of Abraham Lincoln's papers at the Library of Congress in May, 1919. In a deed of gift, signed January 23, 1923, Robert Lincoln stipulated that the papers were to be placed "in a sealed vault or compartment and carefully preserved from official or public inspection or private view until after the expiration of twenty-one (21) years from the date of my death. This condition is imposed by me because said papers contain many references of a private nature to the immediate ancestors of persons now living, which, in my judgment, should not be made public." On January 16, 1926, he modified the condition of the deed to grant his wife, Mary Harlan Lincoln, access to the papers, and gave her authority to decide whether any other person should be allowed to examine them. Katherine Helm, daughter of Robert Todd Lincoln's aunt, Emily Todd Helm, was the only person given access to the Lincoln papers while the restriction was in force. Miss Helm was the author of *The True Story of Mary, Wife of Lincoln*, published in 1928. The Lincoln papers were opened on July 26, 1947. David C. Mearns, *The Lincoln Papers* (New York, 1948), I, pp. 103–06.

HILDENE, MANCHESTER, VERMONT

August 1st, 1924

Isaac Markens, Esquire
    545 West 64th Street
    New York City
Dear Mr. Markens:

I am in receipt of your letter of the 30th ultimo, congratulating me upon my birthday anniversary, and I wish to thank you for the kind expressions therein contained.

Believe me,

Very truly yours,
Robert T. Lincoln

HILDENE, MANCHESTER, VERMONT

August 8th, 1924

Isaac Markens, Esquire
    545 West 164th Street
    New York City
Dear Mr. Markens:

I am in receipt of your letter of August 5th in regard to my children and their descendants; and, having noted several erroneous statements therein, I am enclosing herewith a brief statement which, as far as it goes, is correct.

Believe me,

Very truly yours,
Robert T. Lincoln

Enclosure

DESCENDANTS OF ROBERT T. LINCOLN

MARY LINCOLN, born October 15th, 1869. Married Charles Isham, of New York, a brother of Samuel Isham, artist. Of this marriage there is one child, Lincoln Isham.

ABRAHAM LINCOLN, born August 14, 1873. Died in London, March 5th, 1890.

JESSIE HARLAN LINCOLN, born November 6th, 1875. Married Warren Beckwith, of which marriage there are two children, Mary and Robert L. Beckwith. Second marriage to Frank Edward Johnson, of Norwich Town, Connecticut.

HILDENE, MANCHESTER, VERMONT

September 19, 1924

Isaac Markens, Esquire
545 West 164th Street
New York City

Dear Sir:

On behalf of Mr. Robert T. Lincoln I beg to acknowledge receipt of your letter of the 15th instant, in which you ask Mr. Lincoln to advise you whether certain statements therein contained concerning Mr. Lincoln's father are correct.

Mr. Lincoln is not in good health at the present time, and he has directed me to write to you and ask that you excuse him from taking up the matter.

Very truly yours,
F. N. Towers
Secretary

HILDENE, MANCHESTER, VERMONT

August 25, 1925

Isaac Markens, Esq.
    545 W. 164th St.
    New York City
Dear Sir:

At the direction of Mr. Robert Lincoln I beg to acknowledge receipt of yours of August 21st. Mr. Lincoln has asked me to say to you that he has no objection to your using any information contained in his various letters to you;—provided, always, of course, such information is not enlarged upon to any considerable extent and is quoted correctly.

As for the picture of his son, Mr. Lincoln has none which he can part with. When you made a request in this same connection some time ago, Mr. Lincoln wrote to you and advised you that he had no picture of his son which he could send you; and the situation has not changed since then. But perhaps you did not receive the letter, or do not recall his having so advised you.

Very truly yours,
F. N. Towers

HILDENE, MANCHESTER, VERMONT

October 16th, 1925

Mr. Isaac Markens
    545 West 164th Street
    New York City
Dear Sir:

At the direction of Mr. Robert Lincoln I acknowledge receipt of your letter of the 15th instant. Mr. Lincoln has asked me to say to you, in reply to your query, that the letter to which you *refer* is not among the papers heretofore deposited by him in the Library of Congress.

Believe me, for Mr. Lincoln,

Very truly yours,
F. N. Towers

HILDENE, MANCHESTER, VERMONT

August 18th, 1926

Isaac Markens, Esq.
    Hotel Regent
    Newark, N.J.
My dear Sir:

Your letter of the 15th instant, in which you ask that I send you "desired information relating to incomplete data in correspondence between Mr. Lincoln and yourself" has come duly to hand.

In reply, I beg to advise you that Mr. Lincoln, during his lifetime,[91] gave you as much information as he thought advisable, and although I note on looking up the file that there are certain queries contained in your various letters remaining unanswered, it would seem clear that, under present circumstances, it would be both improper and impossible for me to endeavor to give you any information which Mr. Lincoln, during his lifetime, did not see fit to communicate to you.

Trusting that you understand my position in this matter, I am,

Very truly yours,
F. N. Towers

91. Robert Todd Lincoln died on July 26, 1926.

INDEX

Herndon, William H.
  and "angel mother" story, 40 n. 36
  charged with malice and lies, 3 n. 1, 7 n. 7
  Robert Lincoln's distrust of, 64
Hertz, Emanuel, on Markens' writings, xii
Hibben, John Grier, Markens criticizes, 64 and n. 75
Holland, J. G.
  Life of Abraham Lincoln, 29 and n. 24
  and origin of sobriquet, "Honest Abe," 30
"Honest Abe" (book title)
  Markens on, 46
  publication of, 34 n. 30
  Robert Lincoln has no interest in, 57
  title proposed, 24–33
"Honest Abe" (sobriquet), origin of, 24 n. 22, 29 and n. 24, 30
Houghton Mifflin Co., to publish Rothschild book, 25–33
Hunter, R. M. T., at Hampton Roads conference, 45 n. 46

Illinois State Historical Library, has copy of Gettysburg Address, 17 n. 16
Illinois State Library, 46–47
Illinois State Republican Convention, mentioned, 28 n. 23
Isham, Charles, marries Mary Lincoln, 82
Isham, Lincoln, grandson of Robert Lincoln, 82

Jews, in America, ix–x
Johnson, Andrew
  inaugural address, 74–75
  and vice-presidency, 56 n. 62
Johnson, Frank Edward, second husband of Jessie Harlan Lincoln, 82

Keely, James, letter to, about photograph, xii n. 3
Kellogg, William Pitt
  appointed Collector of Port of New Orleans, 76 and n. 88
  career of, 48 n. 48
  mentioned, 46

Lamon, Ward Hill, malice of, 3 n. 1
Lee, Robert E., escape from Gettysburg angers Lincoln, 64
Leet Brothers, photograph of Lincoln, 76 and n. 87
Library of Congress
  has copies of Gettysburg Address, 17 n. 16, 50 n. 51
  holds Lincoln papers in trust, 80 and n. 90
Lincoln, Abraham (grandfather of the President), estate of 59 and n. 67
Lincoln, Abraham (the President)
  alleged conversion of, 10–13 and notes 11 and 12

This book and jacket-wrap have been designed
by Michael Stancik. The text has been set in monotype
Janson which was faithfully cast and recut
from the original matrices by Anton Janson
between 1660 and 1687. The body paper used is
white Mohawk superfine text, eggshell finish and
was manufactured by the Mohawk Paper Mills, Inc.,
Cohoes, New York. The linen finish cloth for the
binding was manufactured by Joseph Bancroft & Sons
Company, New York, New York. The typesetting,
printing and binding were performed at
The Lakeside Press, R. R. Donnelley & Sons Company,
Chicago, Illinois and Crawfordsville, Indiana.